The Chymical Marriage Of Christian

Rosencreutz

Arthur Edward Waite

Kessinger Publishing's Rare Reprints

Thousands of Scarce and Hard-to-Find Books on These and other Subjects!

- Americana
- Ancient Mysteries
- Animals
- Anthropology
- Architecture
- Arts
- Astrology
- Bibliographies
- Biographies & Memoirs
- Body, Mind & Spirit
- Business & Investing
- Children & Young Adult
- Collectibles
- Comparative Religions
- Crafts & Hobbies
- Earth Sciences
- Education
- Ephemera
- Fiction
- Folklore
- Geography
- Health & Diet
- History
- Hobbies & Leisure
- Humor
- Illustrated Books
- Language & Culture
- Law
- Life Sciences
- Literature
- Medicine & Pharmacy
- Metaphysical
- Music
- Mystery & Crime
- Mythology
- Natural History
- Outdoor & Nature
- Philosophy
- Poetry
- Political Science
- Science
- Psychiatry & Psychology
- Reference
- Religion & Spiritualism
- Rhetoric
- Sacred Books
- Science Fiction
- Science & Technology
- Self-Help
- Social Sciences
- Symbolism
- Theatre & Drama
- Theology
- Travel & Explorations
- War & Military
- Women
- Yoga
- *Plus Much More!*

We kindly invite you to view our catalog list at:
http://www.kessinger.net

CHAPTER V.

THE CHYMICAL MARRIAGE OF CHRISTIAN ROSENCREUTZ.

THE whole Rosicrucian controversy centres in this publication, which Buhle describes as "a comic romance of extraordinary talent." It was first published at Strasbourg in
the year 1616, but, as will be seen in the seventh chapter,
it is supposed to have existed in manuscript as early as
1601-2, thus antedating by a long period the other Rosicrucian books. Two editions of the German original are
preserved in the Library of the British Museum, both bearing the date 1616.[1] It was translated into English for the
first time in 1690, under the title of "The Hermetic
Romance: or The Chymical Wedding. Written in High
Dutch by Christian Rosencreutz. Translated by E. Fox-
croft, late Fellow of King's Colledge in Cambridge.
Licensed and entered according to Order. Printed by A.
Sowle, at the Crooked Billet in Holloway-Lane, Shoreditch;
and Sold at the Three-Keys in Nags-Head-Court, Grace-
church-street." It is this translation in substance, that
is, compressed by the omission of all irrelevant matter and
dispensable prolixities, which I now offer to the reader.

[1] "Chymische Hochzeit: Christiani Rosencreutz. Anno 1459.
Erstlick Gedrucktzor Strasbourg. Anno M.DC.XVI." The second
edition was printed by Conrad Echer.

The Chymical Marriage of Christian Rosencreutz.   Anno 1459.

Arcana publicata vilescunt, et gratiam prophanata amittunt.
Ergo: ne Margaritas objice porcis, seu Asino substernere rosas.

THE FIRST BOOK.

The First Day.

Meditatio.

On an evening before Easter-day, I sate at a table, and having in my humble prayer conversed with my Creator and considered many great mysteries (whereof the Father of Lights had shewn me not a few), and being now ready to prepare in my heart, together with my dear Paschal Lamb, a small, unleavened, undefiled cake, all on a sudden ariseth so horrible a tempest, that I imagined no other but that, through its mighty force, the hill whereon my little house was founded would fly all in pieces.   But inasmuch as this, and the like, from the devil (who had done me many a spight) was no new thing to me, I took courage, and persisted in my meditation till somebody touched me on the back, whereupon I was so hugely terrified that I durst hardly look about me, yet I shewed myself as cheerful as humane frailty would permit.   Now the same thing still twitching me several times by the coat, I glanced back and behold it was

Praeconissa

a fair and glorious lady, whose garments were all skye-colour, and curiously bespangled with golden stars.   In her right hand she bare a trumpet of beaten gold, whereon a Name was ingraven which I could well read but am forbidden as yet to reveal.   In her left hand she had a great bundle of letters in all languages, which she (as I afterwards understood) was to carry into all countries.   She had also large and beautiful wings, full of eyes throughout, wherewith she could mount aloft, and flye swifter than any eagle. As soon as I turned about, she looked through her letters, and at length drew out a small one, which, with great reverence, she laid upon the table, and, without one word, departed from me. But in her mounting upward, she gave so mighty a blast on her gallant trumpet that the whole hill echoed thereof, and for a full quarter of an hour afterward I could hardly hear my own words.

In so unlooked for an adventure I was at a loss how to advise myself, and, therefore, fell upon my knees, and besought my Creator to permit nothing contrary to my eternal happiness to befall me, whereupon, with fear and trembling, I went to the letter, which was now so heavy as almost to *Epistola.* outweigh gold. As I was diligently viewing it, I found a little Seal, whereupon was ingraven a curious Cross, with *Sigillum*

this inscription IN HOC SIGNO ⟨symbol⟩ VINCES.

As soon as I espied this sign I was comforted, not being ignorant that it was little acceptable, and much less useful, to the devil. Whereupon I tenderly opened the letter, and within it, in an azure field, in golden letters, found the following verses written :—

> " This day, this day, this, this
>   The Royal Wedding is.
> Art thou thereto by birth inclined,
> And unto joy of God design'd ?
> Then may'st thou to the mountain tend
> Whereon three stately Temples stand,
> And there see all from end to end.
>   Keep watch and ward,
>   Thyself regard ;
> Unless with diligence thou bathe,
> The Wedding can't thee harmless save :
> He'll damage have that here delays ;
> Let him beware too light that weighs."

Underneath stood *Sponsus* and *Sponsa*.

De Nuptiis.

As soon as I read this letter, I was like to have fainted away, all my hair stood on end, and cold sweat trickled down my whole body. For although I well perceived that this was the appointed wedding whereof seven years before I was acquainted in a bodily vision, and which I had with great earnestness attended, and which, lastly, by the account and calculation of the plannets, I found so to be, yet could

Requisita in hospitibus. Secundum, 7. Pondera.

I never fore-see that it must happen under so grievous and perilous conditions. For whereas I before imagined that to be a well-come guest, I needed onely to appear at the wedding, I was now directed to Divine Providence, of which until this time I was never certain. I also found, the more I examined myself, that in my head there was

1. Electio incerta.

onely gross misunderstanding, and blindness in mysterious things, so that I was not able to comprehend even those

2. Inscitia Ignorantia cæcitas mentis.

things which lay under my feet, and which I daily conversed with, much less that I should be born to the searching out and understanding of the secrets of Nature, since,

3, 4. Naturæ secreta. 5, 6.

in my opinion, Nature might everywhere find a more vertuous disciple, to whom to intrust her precious, though temporary and changeable treasures. I found also that my

Mundana affectio.

bodily behaviour, outward conversation, and brotherly love toward my neighbour was not duly purged and cleansed. Moreover, the tickling of the flesh manifested itself, whose affection was bent only to pomp, bravery, and worldly pride, not to the good of mankind; and I was always contriving how by this art I might in a short time abundantly increase my advantage, rear stately palaces, make myself an everlasting name, and other the like carnal designs. But the obscure words concerning the three Temples did particularly afflict me, which I was not able to make out by any after-speculation. Thus sticking between hope and fear, examining myself again and again, and finding only my own frailty and impotency, and exceedingly amazed at the fore-mentioned threatening, at length I betook myself to my usual course. After I had finished my most fervent prayer, I laid me down in my bed, that so perchance my *Preces.* good angel by the Divine permission might appear, and (as it had formerly happened) instruct me in this affair, which, to the praise of God, did now likewise fall out. For I was yet scarce asleep when me-thought I, together with a num- *Visio per-somnium* berless multitude of men, lay fettered with great chains in a dark dungeon, wherein we swarmed like bees one over *Turris Cæcitas.* another, and thus rendered each other's affliction more grievous. But although neither I, nor any of the rest, could see one jot, yet I continually heard one heaving him-self above the other, when his chains or fetters were become ever so little lighter. Now as I with the rest had con-tinued a good while in this affliction, and each was still reproaching the other with his blindness and captivity, at length we heard many trumpets sounding together, and kettle-drums beating so artificially thereto, that it rejoyced us even in our calamity.

During this noise the cover of the dungeon was lifted up, and a little light let down unto us. Then first might truly *Illustratio.* have been discerned the bustle we kept, for all went pesle-mesle, and he who perchance had too much heaved up him-self was forced down again under the others' feet. In brief, each one strove to be uppermost, neither did I linger, but, with my weighty fetters, slipt from under the rest, and then heaved myself upon a Stone; howbeit, I was several times caught at by others, from whom, as well as I might, I guarded myself with hands and feet. We imagined that we should all be set at liberty, which yet fell out quite otherwise, for after the nobles who looked upon us through the hole had recreated themselves with our struggling, a certain hoary-headed man called to us to be quiet, and, having obtained it, began thus to say on :

Magister carceris.

> If wretched mortals would forbear
>   Themselves to so uphold,
> Then sure on them much good confer
>   My righteous Mother would :
> But since the same will not insue,
> They must in care and sorrow rue,
>   And still in prison lie.
> Howbeit, my dear Mother will
>   Their follies over-see,
> Her choicest goods permitting still
>   Too much in Light to be.
> Wherefore, in honour of the feast
>   We this day solemnize,
> That so her grace may be increast,
>   A good deed she'll devise ;
> For now a cord shall be let down,
> And whosoe'er can hang thereon
>   Shall freely be releast.

Vide S. Bernard, Serm. 3, de 7 Fragmentis

He had scarce done speaking when an Antient Matron commanded her servants to let down the cord seven times into the dungeon, and draw up whomsoever could hang upon it. Good God ! that I could sufficiently describe the hurry that arose amongst us ; every one strove to reach the cord, and only hindred each other. After seven minutes a little bell rang, whereupon at the first pull the servants drew up four. At that time I could not come near the cord, having to my huge misfortune betaken myself to the stone at the wall, whereas the cord descended in the middle. The cord was let down the second time, but divers, because their chains were too heavy, and their hands too tender, could not keep hold on it, and brought down others who else might have

Prima vectura.

Secunda.

held on fast enough. Nay, many were forcibly pulled off by those who could not themselves get at it, so envious were we even in this misery. But they of all most moved my compassion whose weight was so heavy that they tore their hands from their bodies and yet could not get up. Thus it came to pass that at these five times very few were drawn up, for, as soon as the sign was given, the servants were so nimble at the draught that the most part tumbled one upon another. Whereupon, the greatest part, and even myself, despaired of redemption, and called upon God to have pitty on us, and deliver us out of this obscurity, who also heard some of us, for when the cord came down the sixth time, Sexta. some hung themselves fast upon it, and whilst it swung from one side to the other, it came to me, which I suddenly catching, got uppermost, and so beyond all hope came out ; whereat I exceedingly rejoyced, perceiving not the wound which in the drawing up I received on my head by a sharp Vulnus stone, till I, with the rest of the released (as was always exturro Cæcitatis. before done) was fain to help at the seventh and last pull, at Septima. which, through straining, the blood ran down my cloathes. This, nevertheless, through joy I regarded not.

When the last draught, whereon the most of all hung, was finished, the Matron caused the cord to be laid away, and willed her aged son to declare her resolution to the rest Magistræ filius. of the prisoners, who thus spoke unto them.

> Ye children dear
> All present here,
> What is but now compleat and done
> Was long before resolved on ;
> Whate'er my mother of great grace
> To each on both sides here hath shown ;
> May never discontent misplace !
> The joyful time is drawing on

When every one shall equal be—
None wealthy, none in penury.
Whoe'er receiveth great commands
Hath work enough to fill his hands
Whoe'er with much hath trusted been,
'Tis well if he may save his skin ;
Wherefore, your lamentations cease,
What is't to waite for some few dayes ?

The cover was now again put to and locked, the trumpets and kettle-drums began afresh, yet the bitter lamentation of the prisoners was heard above all, and soon caused my eyes to run over. Presently the Antient Matron, together with her son, sate down, and commanded the Redeemed should be told. As soon as she had written down their number in a gold-yellow tablet, she demanded everyone's name ; this was also written down by a little page. Having viewed us all, she sighed, and said to her son—"Ah, how hartily am I grieved for the poor men in the dungeon ! I would to God I durst release them all." Whereunto her son replied—"Mother, it is thus ordained by God, against Whom we may not contend. In case we all of us were lords, and were seated at table, who would there be to bring up the service !" At this his mother held her peace, but soon after she said—" Well, let these be freed from their fetters," which was presently done, and I, though among the last, could not refrain, but bowed myself before the Antient Matron, thanking God that through her had graciously vouchsafed to bring me out of darkness into light. The rest did likewise to the satisfaction of the matron. Lastly, to every one was given a piece of gold for a remembrance, and to spend by the way. On the one side thereof was stamped the rising sun ; on the other these three letters D L S ; therewith all had license to depart to his own business, with this intimation, *that we to the glory of God*

Marginal notes:

Magistra recens et evectos.

Secretarus

Cur non omnes evecti.

Gratitudo auctoris evecti.

Nummus aureus.

Deus Lux solis, vel Deo laus semper.

should benefit our neighbours, and reserve in silence what we had
been intrusted with, which we promised to do, and departed one
from another. Because of the wounds the fetters had caused
me, I could not well go forward, which the matron presently
espying, calling me again to her side, said to me—" My son,
let not this defect afflict thee, but call to mind thy infirmi-
ties, and thank God who hath permitted thee, even in this
world, to come into so high a light. Keep these wounds
for my sake."

Whereupon the trumpets began again to sound, which so
affrighted me that I awoke, and perceived that it was onely
a dream, which yet was so impressed on my imagination
that I was perpetually troubled about it, and methought I
was still sensible of the wounds on my feet. By all these
things I well understood that God had vouchsafed me to be
present at this mysterious and hidden Wedding, wherefore
with childlike confidence I returned thanks to His Divine
Majesty, and besought Him that He would preserve me in
His fear, daily fill my heart with wisdom and understanding, and graciously conduct me to the desired end. Thereupon I prepared myself for the way, put on my white
linnen coat, girded my loyns, with a blood-red ribbon
bound cross-ways over my shoulder. In my hat I stuck
four red roses, that I might the sooner by this token be
taken notice of amongst the throng. For food I took
bread, salt, and water, which by the counsel of an understanding person I had at certain times used, not without
profit, in the like occurrences. Before I parted from my
cottage, I first, in this my wedding garment, fell down upon
my knees, and besought God to vouchsafe me a good issue.
I made a vow that if anything should by His Grace be revealed to me, I would imploy it neither to my own honour

Marginal notes:
Mandatum Taciturnitatis.
Discessus autoris.
Vulnus ex compedibus.
Experget actio.
Solatium.
Precatio.
Præparatio ad iter.
Votum.

nor authority in the world, but to the spreading of His name, and the service of my neighbour.　With this vow I departed out of my cell with joy.

The Second Day.

I was hardly got out of my cell into a forrest when me-thought the whole heaven and all the elements had trimmed themselves against this wedding.　Even the birds chanted more pleasantly then before, and the young fawns skipped so merrily that they rejoiced my old heart, and moved me also to sing with such a loud voice throughout the whole forrest, that it resounded from all parts, the hills repeating my last words, until at length I espyed a curious green heath, whither I betook myself out of the forrest.　Upon this heath stood three tall cedars, which afforded an excellent shade, whereat I greatly rejoyced, for, although I had not gone far, my earnest longing made me faint.　As soon as I came somewhat nigh, I espyed a tablet fastened to one of them, on which the following words were written in curious letters :—

God save thee, Stranger !　If thou hast heard anything concerning the nuptials of the King, consider these words. By us doth the Bridegroom offer thee a choice between foure ways, all of which, if thou dost not sink down in the way, can bring thee to his royal court.　The first is short but dangerous, and one which will lead thee into rocky places, through which it will be, scarcely possible to pass. The second is longer, and takes thee circuitously ; it is plain and easy, if by the help of the Magnet, thou turnest neither to left nor right.　The third is that truly royal way which through various pleasures and pageants of our

King, affords thee a joyful journey; but this so far has scarcely been allotted to one in a thousand. By the fourth 4. shall no man reach the place, because it is a consuming way, practicable onely for incorruptible bodys. Choose now which thou wilt of the three, and persevere constantly therein, for know whichsoever thou shalt enter, that is the one destined for thee by immutable Fate, nor canst thou go back therein save at great peril to life. These are the things which we would have thee know, but, ho, beware ! thou knowest not with how much danger thou dost commit thyself to this way, for if thou knowest thyself by the smallest fault to be obnoxious to the laws of our King, I beseech thee, while it is still possible, to return swiftly to thy house by the way which thou camest.

As soon as I had read this writing all my joy vanished, and I, who before sang merrily, began inwardly to lament. For although I saw all three ways before me, and it was Via authoris vouchsafed me to make choice of one, yet it troubled me eligenda. that in case I went the stony and rocky way, I might get a deadly fall; or, taking the long one, I might wander through bye-ways and be detained in the great journey. Neither durst I hope that I, amongst thousands, should be the one who should choose the Royal way. I saw likewise the fourth before me, but so invironed with fire and exhalation that I durst not draw near it, and, therefore, again and again considered whether I should turn back or take Dubium. one of the ways before me. I well weighed my own unworthiness, and though the dream, that I was delivered out of the tower, still comforted me, yet I durst not confidently Comfirmatio. rely upon it. I was so perplexed that, for great weariness, hunger and thirst seized me, whereupon I drew out my bread, cut a slice of it, which a snow-white dove, of whom

Columba
alba arbori
mercuriali
insidens.

I was not aware, sitting upon the tree, espyed and therewith came down, betaking herself very familiarly to me, to whom I willingly imparted my food, which she received, and with her prettiness did again a little refresh me. But

Corvus
niger.

as soon as her enemy, a most black Raven, perceived it, he straight darted down upon the dove, and taking no notice of me, would needs force away her meat, who could not otherwise guard herself but by flight. Whereupon, both

Versus
Meridiem.

together flew toward the South, at which I was so hugely incensed and grieved, that without thinking, I made haste after the filthy Raven, and so, against my will, ran into one of the fore-mentioned ways a whole field's length. The Raven being thus chased away, and the Dove delivered, I first observed what I had inconsiderately done, and that I was

Autor in
cidit in
2 viam
incogitanter.

already entered into a way, from which, under peril of punishment, I durst not retire, and though I had still wherewith to comfort myself, yet that which was worst of all was, that I had left my bag and bread at the Tree, and could never retrieve them, for as soon as I turned myself about, a contrary wind was so strong against me that it was ready to fell me, but if I went forward, I perceived no hindrance, wherefore I patiently took up my cross, got upon my feet, and resolved I would use my utmost endeavour to get to my journey's end before night. Now, although many apparent

Compassus.

byways showed themselves, I still proceeded with my compass, and would not budge one step from the meridian line. Howbeit, the way was oftentimes so rugged that I was in no little doubt of it. I constantly thought upon the Dove and Raven, and yet could not search out the meaning, until

Diversorium.

upon a high hill afar off I espyed a stately Portal, to which,

Occasus.

not regarding that it was distant from the way I was in, I

⊙

hasted, because the sun had already hid himself under the

hills, and I could elsewhere see no abiding place, which I verily ascribe only to God, Who might have permitted me to go forward, and withheld my eyes that so I might have gazed beside this gate, to which I now made mighty haste, and reached it by so much daylight as to take a competent view of it. It was an exceeding Royal, beautiful Portal, whereon were carved a multitude of most noble figures and devices, every one of which (as I afterwards learned) had its peculiar signification. Above was fixed a pretty large Tablet, with these words, "*Procul hinc procul ite profani,*" and more that I was forbidden to relate. As soon as I was come unto the portal, there streight stepped forth one in a sky-coloured habit, whom I saluted in friendly manner. Though he thankfully returned my greeting, he instantly demanded my Letter of Invitation. O how glad was I that I had brought it with me ! How easily might I have forgotten it as chanced to others, as he himself told me. I quickly presented it, wherewith he was not only satisfied, but showed me abundance of respect, saying, "Come in, my Brother, an acceptable guest you are to me," withal entreating me not to withhold my name from him.

Having replied that I was a Brother of the RED ROSIE CROSS, he both wondred and seemed to rejoyce at it, and then proceeded thus :—" My brother, have you nothing about you wherewith to purchase a token ? " I answered my ability was small, but if he saw anything about me he had a mind to, it was at his service. Having requested of me my bottle of water, and I granting it, he gave me a golden token, whereon stood these letters, S.C., entreating me that when it stood me in good stead, I would remember him. After which I asked him how many were got in before me, which he also told me ; and lastly, out of meer friendship, gave me a

[marginal notes:]
Tabula inscriptionis.

Portitor.

Literæ convocationis.

Nomen authoris.

Emitur aqua Tessera.

Sanctitati constantia sponsus charus. Spes charitas.

Diploma.

sealed letter to the second Porter. Having lingered some time with him, the night grew on, whereupon a great beacon upon the gate was immediately fired, that if any were still upon the way, he might make haste thither. The road where it finished at the castle was enclosed with

Castillum.

walls, and planted with all sorts of excellent fruit trees. On every third tree on each side lanterns were hung up, wherein all the candles were lighted with a glorious torch

Virgo
lucifera.

by a beautiful Virgin, habited in skye-colour, which was so noble and majestic a spectacle that I delayed longer then

The Lady
Chamberlain

was requisite. At length, after an advantageous instruction, I departed from the first porter, and so went on the way, until I came to the second gate, which was adorned

Porta
secunda.
Tabella.

with images and mystick significations. In the affixed Tablet stood—*Date et dabitur volis.* Under this gate lay a

Custos Leo.

terrible Lyon, chained, who, as soon as he espied me, arose and made at me with great roaring, whereupon the second

2 Portitor.

porter, who lay upon a stone of marble, awaked, and wishing me not to be troubled nor affrighted, drove back the lyon, and having received the letter, which I reached him with trembling hand, he read it, and with great respect spake thus to me :—" Now well-come in God's name unto me the man whom of long time I would gladly have seen !''

Meanwhile, he also drew out a token, and asked me whether

Tessera
empta sale.

I could purchase it. But I, having nothing else left but my salt, presented it to him, which he thankfully accepted.

Studio
merentis
Sal humor
Sponso
mittendus
Sal mineralis
Sal
menstrualis.

Upon this token again stood two letters, namely, S.M. Being just about to discourse with him, it began to ring in the castle, whereupon the porter counselled me to run apace, or all the paines I had taken would serve to no purpose, for the lights above began already to be extinguished, whereupon I dispatched with much haste that I heeded not the porter; the virgin, after whom all the lights were put out, was at my heels, and I should never have found the way, had not she with her torch afforded me some light. I was more-over constrained to enter the *Porta clauditur.* very next to her, and the gates were so suddenly clapt to that a part of my coate was locked out, which I was forced to leave behind me, for neither I nor they who stood ready without and called at the gate could prevail with the porter to open it again. He delivered the keys to the virgin, who took them with her into the court. I again surveyed the gate, which now appeared so rich that the world could not equal it. Just by the door were two columns, on one of which *Pyramides portæ.* stood a pleasant figure with this inscription, *Congratulor.* On the other side was a statue with countenance veiled, and beneath was written, *Condoleo.* In brief, the inscriptions and figures thereon were so dark and mysterious that the most dexterous man could not have expounded them, yet all these I shall e'er long publish and explain. Under *Promissum authoris.* this gate I was again to give my name, which was written down in a little vellum-book, and immediately with the rest dispatched to the Lord Bridegroom. Here I first received the true guest-token, which was somewhat less than the former, but much heavier; upon this stood the letters S. P. N. Besides this, a new pair of shoes were given me, *Salus per naturam sponsi præ sentandus nuptiis.* for the floor of the castle was pure shining marble. My old ones I was to give to one of the poor who sate in throngs under the gate. I bestowed them on an old man, after which two pages with as many torches conducted me *Comes puer.* into a little room, where they willed me to sit down upon a form, and, sticking their torches in two holes made in the pavement, they departed, and left me sitting alone. Soon after I heard a noise but saw nothing; it proved to be cer-

H

tain men who stumbled in upon me, but since I could see nothing I was fain to suffer and attend what they would do with me. Presently finding that they were barbers I intreated them not to jostle me, for I was content to do what they desired, whereupon one of them, whom I yet could not see, gently cut away the hair from the crown of my head, but on my forehead, ears, and eyes he permitted my ice-grey locks to hang. In this first encounter I was ready to despair, for, inasmuch as some of them shoved me so forceably, and were still invisible, I could onely think that God for my curiosity had suffered me to miscarry. The unseen barbers carefully gathered up the hair which was cut off, and carried it away. Then the two pages re-entered and heartily laughed at me for being so terrified. They had scarce spoken a few words with me when again a little bell began to ring, which (as the pages informed me) was to give notice for assembling, whereupon they willed me to rise, and through many walks, doors, and winding stairs lighted me into a spacious hall, where there was a great multitude of guests—emperors, kings, princes, and lords, noble and ignoble, rich and poor, and all sorts of people, at which I hugely marvelled, and thought to myself, " Ah ! how gross a fool hast thou been to ingage upon this journey with so much bitterness and toil, when here are fellows whom thou well knowest, and yet hadst never any reason to esteem, while thou, with all thy prayers and supplications, art hardly got in at last."

This and more the devil at that time injected. Meantime one or other of my acquaintance spake to me :—" Oh ! Brother Rosencreutz, art thou here too ? " " Yea, my brethren," I replied, " The grace of God hath helped me in also," at which they raised a mighty laughter, looking upon

Marginal notes:

Balneatores.

Capillus detonsus asservatus.

Pueri bini.

Triclinium.

it as ridiculous that there should be need of God in so slight an occasion. Having demanded each of them concerning his way, and finding most of them were forced to clamber over the rocks, certain invisible trumpets began to sound to the table, whereupon all seated themselves, every one as he judged himself above the rest, so that for me and some other sorry fellows there was hardly a little nook left at the lowermost table. Presently the two pages entred, and one of them said grace in so handsom and excellent a manner as rejoyced the very heart in my body. Howbeit, some made but little reckoning of them, but fleired and winked one at another, biting their lips within their hats, and using like unseemly gestures. After this, meat was brought in, and, albeit none could be seen, everything was so orderly managed that it seemed as if every guest had his proper attendant. Now my Artists having somewhat recruted themselves, and the wine having a little removed shame from their hearts, they presently began to vaunt of their abilities. One would prove this, another that, and commonly the most sorry idiots made the loudest noise. When I call to mind what preternatural and impossible enterprises I then heard, I am still ready to vomit at it. In fine, they never kept in their order, but whenever possible a rascal would insinuate himself among the nobles. Every man had his own prate, and yet the great lords were so simple that they believed their pretences, and the rogues became so audacious, that although some of them were rapped .over the fingers with a knife, yet they flinched not at it, but when any one perchance had filched a gold-chain, then would all hazard for the like. I saw one who heard the movements of the Heavens, the second could see Plato's Ideas, a third could number the atoms of Demo-

Impietas hostum non recta via ingressorum.

Quidam preces negligunt.

Commessatio.

Ministri invisibles.

Inebriatorum gloriatio vana.

critus.   There were not a few pretenders to perpetual motion.   Many an one (in my opinion) had good understanding, but assumed too much to himself to his own destruction.   Lastly, there was one who would needs persuade us that he saw the servitors who attended, and would have pursued his contention, had not one of those invisible waiters reached him so handsom a cuff upon his lying muzzle, that not only he, but many who were by him, became mute as mice.   It best of all pleased me that those of whom I had any esteem were very quiet in their business, acknowledging themselves to be misunderstanding men for whom the mysteries of nature were too high.   In this tumult I had almost cursed the day wherein I came hither, for I could not but with anguish behold that those lewd people were above at the board, but 1 in my sorry place could not even rest in quiet, one of these rascals scornfully reproaching me for a motley fool.   I dreamed not that there was one gate behind through which we must pass, but imagined during the whole wedding I was to continue in this scorn and indignity which I had at no time deserved, either of the Lord Bride-groom or the Bride. And, therefore, I opined he would have done well to seek some other fool than me for his wedding.   To such impatience doth the iniquity of this world reduce simple hearts. But this was really one part of the lameness whereof I had dreamed.

The longer all this clamour lasted, the more it increased. Howbeit, there sate by me a very fine, quiet man, who discoursed of excellent matters, and at length said : —" My Brother, if any one should come now who were willing to instruct these blockish people in the right way, would he be heard ? "   " No, verily," I replyed.   " The world," said

Marginal notes:

Ministri invisibles.

Modestia proborum hospitum.

Impatientia ex iniquitate hominum.

Assessor modestus.

he, " is now resolved to be cheated, and will give no ear to those who intend its good. Seest thou that Cock's-comb, with what whimsical figures and foolish conceits he allures others. There one makes mouths at the people with un-heard-of mysterious words. Yet the time is now coming when those shameful vizards shall be plucked off, and the world shall know what vagabond imposters were concealed behind them. Then perhaps that will be valued which at present is not esteemed." *Mundus valt decipi.*

While he was thus speaking, and the clamour was still increasing, all on a sudden there began in the hall such ex-cellent and stately musick of which, all the days of my life, I never heard the like. Every one held his peace, and at-tended what would come of it. There were all stringed instruments imaginable, sounding together in such har-mony that I forgot myself, and sate so unmovably that those by me were amazed. This lasted nearly half an hour, wherein none of us spake one word, for as soon as anyone was about to open his mouth, he got an unexpected blow. After that space this musick ceased suddenly, and presently before the door of the hall began a great sounding and beating of trumpets, shalms, and kettle-drums, all so master-like as if the Emperor of Rome had been entring. The door opened of itself, and then the noise of the trum-pets was so loud that we were hardly able to indure it. Meanwhile, many thousand small tapers came into the hall, marching of themselves in so exact an order as amazed us, till at last the two fore-mentioned pages with bright torches entred lighting in a most beautiful Virgin, drawn on a gloriously gilded, triumphant self-moving throne. She seemed to me the same who on the way kindled and put out the lights, and that these her attendants were the *Musica.* *Mulctæ ab attendentium* *Faculæ ad lectum.* *Virgo luci-fera.* *The Lady Chamberlain*

Albedo.

very ones whom she formerly placed at the trees. She was not now in skye-colour, but in a snow-white, glittering robe, which sparkled of pure gold, and cast such a lustre that we durst not steadily behold it. Both the pages were after the same manner habited, albeit somewhat more slightly. As soon as they were come into the middle of the hall, and were descended from the throne, all the small tapers made obeisance before her, whereupon we all stood up, and she having to us, as we again to her, shewed all

Salutatoria hospitum.

respect and reverence, in a most pleasant tone she began thus to speak :—

> " The King my Lord most gracious,
> Who now's not very far from us,
> As also his most lovely Bride,
> To him in troth and honour tied,
> Already, with great joy indued,
> Have your arrival hither view'd ;
> And do to every one and all
> Promise their grace in special ;
> And from their very heart's desire
> You may the same in time acquire,
> That so their future nuptial joy
> May mixed be with none's annoy."

Hereupon, with all her small tapers, she again courteously bowed, and presently began thus :—

Propositio actionis.

> " In th' Invitation writ you know
> That no man called was hereto
> Who of God's rarest gifts good store
> Had not received long before.
> Although we cannot well conceit
> That any man's so desperate,
> Under conditions so hard,
> Here to intrude without regard,
> Unless he have been first of all
> Prepared for this Nuptial,
> And, therefore, in good hopes do dwell
> That with all you it will be well ;

Yet men are grown so bold and rude,
Not weighing their ineptitude,
As still to thrust themselves in place
Whereto none of them called was.
No cock's-comb here himself may sell,
No rascal in with others steal,
For we resolve without all let
A Wedding pure to celebrate.
So, then, the artists for to weigh,   Probatio
Scales shall be fixt th' ensuing day ;   artificum
Whereby each one may lightly find
What he hath left at home behind.
If here be any of that rout,
Who have good cause themselves to doubt,
Let him pack quickly hence aside,
Because in case he longer bide,
Of grace forelorn, and quite undone,
Betimes he must the gantlet run.
If any now his conscience gall,
He shall to-night be left in th' hall,
And be again release by morn,
Yet so he hither ne'er return.
If any man have confidence,
He with his waiter may go hence,
Who shall him to his chamber light,
Where he may rest in peace to-night."

As soon as she had done speaking, she again made reverence, and sprung chearfully into her throne, after which the trumpets began again to sound, and conducted her invisibly away, but the most part of the small tapers remained, and still one of them accompanied each of us. In our perturbation, 'tis scarcely possible to express what pensive thoughts and gestures were amongst us, yet most part resolved to await the scale, and in case things sorted not well to depart (as they hoped) in peace. I had soon Autor
cast up my reckoning, and seeing my conscience convinced humiliat se.
me of all ignorance and unworthiness, I purposed to stay with the rest in the hall, and chose rather to content myself

with the meal I had taken than to run the risk of a future repulse. After every one by his small taper had been severally conducted to a chamber (each, as I since understood, into a peculiar one), there staid nine of us, including he who discoursed with me at the table. Although our small tapers left us not, yet within an hour's time one of the pages came in, and, bringing a great bundle of cords with him, first demanded whether we had concluded to stay there, which when we had with sighs affirmed, he bound each of us in a several place, and so went away with our tapers, leaving us poor wretches in darkness. Then first began some to perceive the imminent danger, and myself could not refrain tears, for, although we were not forbidden to speak, anguish and affliction suffered none of us to utter one word. The cords were so wonderfully made that none could cut them, much less get them off his feet, yet this comforted me, that the future gain of many an one who had now betaken himself to rest would prove little to his satisfaction, but we by one night's pennance might expiate all our presumption. At length in my sorrowful thoughts I fell asleep, during which I had a *Somnium typicum.* dream which I esteem not impertinent to recount. Methought I was upon an high mountain, and saw before me *What will be the issue of the probatory beam? He that climbs high hath a great fall.* a great valley, wherein were gathered an unspeakable multitude, each of whom had at his head a string by which he was hanging. Now one hung high, another low, some stood even quite upon the earth. In the air there flew up and down an ancient man, who had in his hand a pair of sheers, wherewith here he cut one's and there another's thread. Now he that was nigh the earth fell without noise, but when this happened to the high ones the earth quaked at their fall. To some it came to pass that their thread was so stretched they came to the earth before it was cut. I took pleasure at this tumbling, and it joyed me at the heart when he who had over-exalted himself in the air, of his wedding, got so shameful a fall that it carried even some of his neighbours along with him. In like manner it rejoyced me that he who had kept so near the earth could come down so gently that even his next men perceived it not. But in my highest fit of jollity, I was unawares jogged by one of my fellow-captives, upon which I *Experget.* waked and was much discontented with him. Howbeit, I considered my dream and recounted it to my brother, who lay by me on the other side, and who hoped some comfort might thereby be intended. In such discourse we spent the remaining part of the night, and with longing expected the day.

The Third Day.

As soon as the lovely day was broken, and the bright sun, having raised himself above the hills, had betaken himself to his appointed office, my good champions began to rise and leisurely make themselves ready unto the inquisition. Whereupon, one after another they came again into the hall, and giving us a good morrow, demanded *Colloquium surgentium.* how we had slept; and having espied our bonds, some reproved us for being so cowardly, that we had not, as they, hazarded upon all adventures. Howbeit, some, whose hearts still smote them, made no loud cry of the business. We excused ourselves with our ignorance, hoping we should soon be set at liberty and learn wit by this disgrace, that they also had not altogether escaped, and perhaps their greatest danger was still to be expected. At length all being assembled, the trumpets began again to *Cantus.*

sound and the kettle-drums to beat, and we imagined that the Bride-groom was ready to present himself, which, nevertheless, was a huge mistake, for again it was the Virgin, who had arrayed herself all in red velvet, and girded herself with a white scarfe. Upon her head she had a green wreath of laurel, which much became her. Her train was no more of small tapers, but consisted of two hundred men in harness, all cloathed, like herself, in red and white. As soon as they were alighted from the throne, she comes streight to us prisoners, and, after she had saluted us, said in few words :—"That some of you have been sensible of your wretched condition is pleasing to my most mighty Lord, and he is also resolved you shall fare the better for it." Having espied me in my habit, she laughed and spake :—"Good lack! Hast thou also submitted thyself to the yoke! I imagined thou wouldst have made thyself very snug," which words caused my eyes to run over. After this she commanded we should be unbound, cuppled together, and placed in a station where we might well behold the scales. "For," said she, "it may fare better with them than with the presumptuous who yet stand at liberty."

Meantime the scales, which were intirely of gold, were hung up in the midst of the hall. There was also a little table covered with red velvet, and seven weights thereon—first of all stood a pretty great one, then four little ones, lastly, two great ones severally, and these weights in proportion to their bulk were so heavy that no man can believe or comprehend it. Each of the harnised men carried a naked sword and a strong rope. They were distributed according to the number of weights into seven bands, and out of every band was one chosen for their

Virgo lucifera.
The Lady Chamberlain

Solatur humiles.

Libra aurea.

7. Pondera.

Satellites.

proper weight, after which the Virgin again sprung up into her high throne, and one of the pages commanded each to place himself according to his order, and successively step into the scale. One of the Emperors, making no scruple, first bowed himself a little towards the Virgin, and in all his stately attire went up, whereupon each captain laid in his weight, which (to the wonder of all) he stood out. But the last was too heavy for him, so that forth he must, and that with such anguish that the Virgin herself seemed to pitty him, yet was the good Emperor bound and delivered to the sixth band. Next him came forth another Emperor, who stept hautily into the scale, and, having a thick book under his gown, he imagined not to fail; but, being scarce able to abide the third weight, he was unmercifully slung down, and his book in that affrightment slipping from him, all the soldiers began to laugh, and he was delivered up bound to the third band. Thus it went also with some others of the Emperors, who were all shamefully laughed at and made captive. After these comes forth a little short man, with a curled brown beard, an Emperor too, who, after the usual reverence, got up and held out so stedfastly that methought had there been more weights he would have outstood them. To him the Virgin immediately arose and bowed before him, causing him to put on a gown of red velvet, then reaching him a branch of laurel, whereof she had good store upon her throne, on the steps of which she willed him to sit down. How after him it fared with the rest of the Emperors, Kings, and Lords, would be too long to recount; few of those great personages held out, though sundry eminent vertues were found in many. Everyone who failed was miserably laughed at by the bands. After the inquisition had passed over the

Marginal notes:
Pendesantur artifices.
1. Cæsar.
2. Cæsar.
3. Alii Cæsares.
4. Cæsar.

gentry, the learned, and unlearned, in each condition one, it may be, two, but mostly none, being found perfect, it came to those vagabond cheaters and rascally *Lapidem Spitalanficum* makers, who were set upon the scale with such scorn, that for all my grief I was ready to burst my belly with laughing, neither could the prisoners themselves refrain, for the most part could not abide that severe trial, but with whips and scourges were jerked out of the scale. Thus of so pert a throng so few remained that I am ashamed to discover their number. Howbeit, there were persons of quality also amongst them who, notwithstanding, were also honoured with velvet robes and wreaths of lawrel.

The inquisition being finished, and none but we poor coupled hounds standing aside, one of the captains stept forth, and said :—"Gratious madam, if it please your ladyship, let these poor men, who acknowledged their misunderstanding, be set upon the scale also without danger of penalty, and only for recreation's sake, if perchance anything right be found among them." At this I was in great perplexity, for in my anguish this was my only comfort, that I was not to stand in such ignominy, or be lashed out of the scale. Yet since the Virgin consented, so it must be, and we being untied were one after another set up. Now, although the most part miscarried, they were neither laughed at nor scourged, but peaceably placed on one side. My companion was the fifth, who held out bravely, whereupon all, but especially the captain who made the request for us, applauded him, and the Virgin showed him the usual respect. After him two more were despatched in an instant. But I was the eighth, and as soon as (with trembling) I stepped up, my companion, who already sat

*Proba fal-
sariorum.*

*Nobiles
nihilominus
ornantur.*

*Proba
Humilium.*

*Socius
Autoris.*

Autor.

by in his velvet, looked friendly upon me, and the Virgin
herself smiled a little. But, for as much as I outstayed
all the weights, the Virgin commanded them to draw me up
by force, wherefore three men moreover hung on the other-
side of the beam, and yet could nothing prevail. Whereupon
one of the pages immediately stood up, and cryed out exceeding loud, "THAT IS HE," upon which the other That is he.
replyed :—"Then let him gain his liberty !" which the
Virgin accorded, and being received with due ceremonies,
the choice was given me to release one of the captives,
whomsoever I pleased, whereupon I made no long delibera- Probatissi-
tions, but elected the first Emperor, whom I had long mus.
pittied, who was immediately set free, and with all respect Liberat, 1.
seated among us. Now, the last being set up the weights Cæsarem.
proved too heavy for him ; meanwhile the Virgin espied my
roses, which I had taken out of my hat into my hands, and
thereupon by her page graciously requested them of me, Autor rosam
suam donat
which I readily sent her. And so this first act was finished virgini.
about ten in the forenoon. Hora, 10.
Actus.

The trumpets again began to sound, which, nevertheless,
we could not as yet see. Meantime the bands were to step
aside with their prisoners and expect the judgment, after
which a council of the seven captains and ourselves was set,
with the Virgin as president, whereat it was concluded that
all the principal lords should with befitting respect be led Judicium de
reprobatis.
out of the castle, that others should be stripped and caused
to run out naked, while others yet with rods, whips, or
dogs, should be hunted out. Those who the day before
willingly surrendered themselves might be suffered to depart without any blame, but those presumptuous ones, and
they who had behaved themselves so unseemly at dinner,
should be punished in body and life according to each

man's demerit. This opinion pleased the Virgin well, and obtained the upper hand. There was moreover another dinner vouchsafed them, the execution itself being deferred till noon. Herewith the senate arose, and the Virgin, together with her attendants, returned to her usual quarter. The uppermost table in the room was allotted to us till the business was fully dispatched, when we should be conducted to the Lord Bride-groom and Bride, with which we were well content. The prisoners were again brought into *Prandium.*   the hall, and each man seated according to his quality. They were enjoyed to behave somewhat more civilly than they had done the day before, which admonishment they needed not, for they had already put up their pipes, and this I can boldly say, that commonly those who were of highest rank best understood how to comport themselves in so unexpected a misfortune. Their treatment was but indifferent, yet with respect, neither could they see their *Ministri*   attendants, who were visible to us, whereat I was exceed- *invisibles* *visibles.*   ing joyful. Although fortune had exalted us, we took not upon us more than the rest, advising them to be of good cheer, and comforting them as well as we could, drinking with them to try if the wine might make them cheerful. *Proborum*   Our table was covered with red velvet, beset with drinking *exaltatio.*   cups of pure silver and gold, which the rest could not behold without amazement and anguish. Ere we had seated ourselves in came the two pages, presenting every one, in the Bride-groom's behalf, the Golden Fleece with a flying Lyon, requesting us to wear them at the table, and to observe the reputation and dignity of the order which his *Remuneratio* Majesty had vouchsafed us and would ratify with sutable *a-sponso.*   ceremonies. This we received with profoundest submission, promising to perform whatever his Majesty should please.   Beside these, the noble page had a schedule wherein we were set down in order.   Now because our entertainment was exceeding stately, we demanded one of the pages whether we might have leave to send some choice bit to our friends and acquaintance, who making no difficulty, every one sent by the waiters ; howbeit the receivers saw none of them ; and forasmuch as they knew not whence it came, I was myself desirous to carry somewhat to one of them, but, as soon as I was risen, one of the waiters was *Autori denegatur communicatio erga reprobos.* at my elbow, desiring me to take friendly warning, for in case one of the pages had seen it, it would have come to the King's ear, who would certainly take it amiss of me ; but since none had observed it save himself, he purposed not to betray me, and that I must for the time to come have better regard to the dignity of the order.   With these words, the servant did really so astonish me that for long I scarce moved upon my seat, yet I returned him thanks for his faithful warning as well as I was able.   Soon after the drums began to beat, wherefore we prepared ourselves to receive the Virgin, who now came in with her *Virgo lucifera. The Lady Chamberlain.* train, upon her high seat, one of the pages bearing before her a very tall goblet of gold, and the other a patent in parchment.   Being now after a marvellous artificial manner alighted from her seat, she takes the goblet from the page and presents it in the King's behalf, saying that it was brought from his Majesty, and that in honour of him we *Calix obambulans.* should cause it to go round.   Upon the cover of this goblet stood Fortune curiously cast in gold, who had in her hand a red flying ensign, for which cause I drunk somewhat the more sadly, as having been too well acquainted with Fortune's waywardness.   But the Virgin who also was adorned *Ornatus virginis.* with the Golden Fleece and Lyon, hereupon began to distinguish the patent which the other page held into two different parts, out of which thus much was read before the first company :—

Reprobi
dividuntur.

Accusatio
unius partis.

That they should confess that they had too lightly given credit to false, fictitious books, had assumed too much to themselves, and so come into this castle uninvited, and perhaps designing to make their markets here and after-wards to live in the greater pride and lordliness. Thus one had seduced another, and plunged him into disgrace and ignominy, wherefore they were deservedly to be soundly punished—all which they, with great humility, readily acknowledged, and gave their hands upon it, after which a severe check was given to the rest, much to this purpose:—

Affectibus
mundanis

Alterius
partis.

That they were convinced in their consciences of forging false, fictitious books, had befooled and cheated others, thereby diminishing regal dignity amongst all. They knew what ungodly, deceitful figures they had made use of, not even sparing the Divine Trinity. It was also clear as day with what practices they had endeavoured to ensnare the guests; in like manner, it was manifest to all the world that they wallowed in open whoredom, adultery, gluttony, and other uncleannesses. In brief, they had disparaged Kingly Majesty, even amongst the common sort, and there-fore should confess themselves to be convicted vagabond-cheats, and rascals, for which they deserved to be cashiered from the company of civil people, and severely to be punished.

The good Artists were loath to come to this confession, but inasmuch as the Virgin not only herself threatned, and sware their death, but the other party also vehemently raged at them, crying that they had most wickedly seduced them out of the Light, they at length, to prevent a huge misfortune, confessed the same with dolour, yet alledged their actions should not be animadverted upon in the worst Excusatio. sense, for the Lords were resolved to get into the castle, and had promised great sums of money to that effect, each one had used all craft to seize upon something, and so things were brought to the present pass. Thus they had disserved no more than the Lords themselves. Their books also sold so mightily that whoever had no other means to maintain himself was fain to ingage in this consonage. They hoped, moreover, they should be found no way to have miscarried, as having behaved towards the Lords, as became servants, upon their earnest entreaty. But answer was made that his Royal Majesty had determined to punish Refutatio. all, albeit one more severely than another. For although what they had alledged was partly true, and therefore the Lords should not wholly be indulged, yet they had good reason to prepare themselves for death, who had so presumptuously obtruded themselves, and perhaps seduced the ignorant against their will. Thereupon many began most Dolor de sententia. pitteously to lament and prostrate themselves, all which could avail them nothing, and I much marvelled how the Virgin could be so resolute, when their misery caused our eyes to run over. She presently dispatched her page, who brought with him all the cuirassiers which had been appointed at the scales, who were each commanded to take his own man, and, in an orderly procession, conduct him Executio sententi- into her great garden. Leave was given to my yesterday arum companions to go out into the garden unbound, and be present at the execution of the sentence. When every man Spectatores was come forth, the Virgin mounted up into her high throne, requesting us to sit down upon the steps, and appear at the judgment. The goblet was committed to the

I

pages' keeping, and we went forth in our robes upon the throne, which of itself moved so gently as if we had passed in the air, till we came into the garden, where we arose

Hortus.

altogether. This garden was not extraordinarily curious, only it pleased me that the trees were planted in so good order. Besides there ran in it a most costly fountain, adorned with wonderful figures and inscriptions and strange

Autor promittit alter librum.

characters (which, God willing, I shall mention in a future book). In this garden was raised a wooden scaffold, hung with curiously painted figured coverlets. There were four galleries made one over another ; the first was more glorious than the rest and covered with a white Taffata curtain, so that we could not perceive who was behind it. The second was empty and uncovered, while the two last were draped with red and blew Taffata. As soon as we were come to the scaffold the Virgin bowed herself down to the ground, at which we were mightily terrified, for we could easily guess that the King and Queen must not be far off. We also having duely performed our reverence, the Virgin led us by the winding stairs into the second gallery, where she placed herself uppermost, and us in our former order.

Gratitudo Cæsaris erga liberatorem.

But how the emperor whom I had released behaved towards me, I cannot relate for fear of slander, for he might well imagine in what anguish he now should have been, and that only through me he had attained such dignity and worthiness. Meantime, the virgin who first brought me the invitation, and whom I had hitherto never since seen, stepped in, and giving one blast upon her trumpet declared the sentence with a very loud voice :—

Oratio ad judicados.

"The King's Majesty, my most gratious Lord, could from his heart wish that all here assembled had, upon his Majestie's invitation, presented themselves so qualified that they might have adorned his nuptial and joyous Feast. But since it hath otherwise pleased Almighty God, he hath not wherewith to murmur, but is forced, contrary to his inclination, to abide by the antient and laudable constitutions of this Kingdom, albeit, that his Majesty's clemency may be celebrated, the usual sentence shall be considerably lenified. He vouchsafes to the Lords and Potentates not *Sententia magnatum* only their lives intirely, but also freely dismisses them, courteously intreating your Lordships not to take it in evil part that you cannot be present at his Feast of Honour. Neither is your reputation hereby prejudiced, although you be rejected by this our Order, since we cannot at once do all things, and forasmuch as your Lordships have been seduced by base rascals, it shall not pass unrevenged. Furthermore, his Majesty resolveth shortly to communicate with you a Catalogue of Hereticks, or Index Expurgatorius, that you may with better judgment discern between good and evil. And because his Majesty also purposeth to rummage his library, and offer the seductive writings to Vulcan, he courteously entreats every one of you to put the same in execution with your own, whereby it is to be hoped that all evil and mischief may be remedied. And you are admonished never henceforth so inconsiderately to covet entrance hither, least the former excuse of seducers be taken from you. In fine, as the estates of the Land have still somewhat to demand of your Lordships, his Majesty hopes that no man will think it much to redeem himself with a chain, or what else he hath about him, and so, in friendly manner, depart from us.

"The others who stood not at the first, third, and fourth *Sententia, 2* weight, his Majesty will not so lightly dismiss, but that they also may experience his gentleness, it is his command to strip them naked, and so send them forth. Those who

3

in the second and fifth weight were found too light shall, besides stripping, be noted with one or more brands, according as each was lighter or heavier. They who were

4.

drawn up by the sixth or seventh shall be somewhat more gratiously dealt with, and so forward, for unto every combination there is a certain punishment ordained. They

5.

who yesterday separated themselves of their own accord

6.

shall go at liberty without blame. Finally, the convicted vagabond-cheats, who could move up none of the weights, shall be punished, in body and life, with sword, halter, water, and rods, and such execution of judgment shall be inviolably observed for an example unto others."

Finis habiti
judici.

Herewith one virgin broke her wand; the other, who read the sentence, blew her trumpet, and stepped with profound reverence towards the curtain. Now this judgment

Reorum
mores.

being read over, the Lords were well satisfied, for which cause they gave more than they were desired, each one redeeming himself with chains, jewels, gold, monies, and

Ministrorum
mores.

other things, and with reverence they took leave. Although the King's servants were forbidden to jear any at his departure, some unlucky birds could not hold laughing, and certainly it was sufficiently ridiculous to see them pack away with such speed, without once looking behind them. At the door was given to each of them a draught of FOR-

Haustus
oblivionis.

GETFULNESS, that he might have no further memory of misfortune. After these the volunteers departed, who, because of their ingenuity, were suffered to pass, but so as never to return in the same fashion, albeit if to them (as likewise to the others) anything further were revealed, they should be well-come guests.

Damnati.

Meanwhile, others were stripping, in which also an

inequality, according to demerit, was observed. Some were sent away naked, without other hurt; others were driven out with small bells; some again were scourged forth. In brief, the punishments were so various, that I am not able to recount them all. With the last a somewhat longer time was spent, for whilst some were hanging, some beheading, some forced to leap into the water, much time was consumed. Verily, at this execution my eyes ran over, not indeed in regard of the punishment which impudency well deserved, but in contemplation of human blindness, in that we are continually busying ourselves over that which since the first fall hath been sealed to us. Thus the garden which lately was quite full was soon emptied. _{Commiserationis} As soon as this was done, and silence had been kept for _{expositio.} the space of five minutes, there came forward a beautiful snow-white Unicorn, with a golden collar, ingraved with _{Unicorna.} certain letters, about his neck. He bound himself down upon his fore-feet, as if hereby he had shown honour to the Lyon, who stood so immoveably upon the fountain that I _{Leo.} took him to be stone or brass, but who immediately took the naked sword which he bare in his paw, brake it into _{Machæra.} two in the middle, the two pieces whereof sunk into the fountain, after which he so long reared until a white Dove _{Columba.} brought a branch of olive in her bill, which the Lyon devoured in an instant, and so was quieted. The Unicorn returned to his place with joy, while our Virgin led us down by the winding staires from the scaffold, and so we again made our reverence towards the curtain. We washed _{Discessus} our hands and heads in the fountain, and thereby waited _{ab hoc actu.} in order till the King through a secret gallery returned into his hall, and then we also, with choice musick, pomp, state, and pleasant discourse, were conducted into our former lodging.   Here, that the time might not seem too long to us, the Virgin bestowed on each of us a noble Page, not only richly habited but also exceeding learned, and able aptly to discourse on all subjects, so that we had reason to be ashamed of ourselves.   These were commanded to lead us up and down the castle, yet only in certain places, and, if possible, to shorten the time according to our desire.

Discessus virgini luciferæ.

Meantime, the Virgin took leave, promising to be with us again at supper, and after that to celebrate the ceremonies of hanging up the weights, while on the morrow we should

Hospitum modi in delecta-mentis.

be presented to the King.   Each of us now did what best pleased him, one part viewing the excellent paintings, which they copied for themselves, and considered what the wonderful characters might signify, others recruiting them-

Autoris.

selves with meat and drink.   I caused my Page to conduct me, with my Companion, up and down the castle, of which walk it will never repent me so long as I live.   Besides many other glorious antiquities, the Royal Sepulcher was shewed me, by which I learned more than is extant in all books.   There in the same place stands the glorious Phœ-

Libellus de Phœnice.

nix, of which two years since I published a small discourse, and am resolved, in case this narrative prove useful, to set forth several treatises concerning the Lyon, Eagle, Griffon, Falcon, &c., together with their draughts and inscriptions. It grieves me also for my other consorts that they neglected such pretious treasures.   I indeed reaped the most benefit by my Page, for according as each one's genius lay, so he led his intrusted one into the quarters pleasing to him.

Usus eorum quæ autor vidit.

Now the kyes hereunto belonging were committed to my Page, and, therefore, this good fortune happened to me before the rest, for though he invited others to come in, yet they imagining such tombs to be only in the churchyard, thought they should well enough get thither when ever anything was to be seen there. Neither shall these monuments be with-held from my thankful schollars. The other thing that was shewed us two was the noble Library Bibliotheca. as it was altogether before the Reformation, of which I have so much the less to say, because the catalogue is shortly to be published. At the entry of this room stands a great Book the like whereof I never saw, in which all the figures, rooms, portals, writings, riddles, and the like, to be seen in the whole castle are delineated. In every book stands its author painted, whereof many were to be burnt, that even their memory might be blotted out from amongst the righteous. Having taken a full view, and being scarce gotten forth, there comes another Page, and having whispered somewhat in our Page's ear, he delivered up the kyes to him, who immediately carried them up the winding stairs; but our Page was very much out of countenance, and we, setting hard upon him with intreaties, he declared to us that the King's Majesty would by no means permit that either the library or sepulchers should be seen by man, and he besought us as we tendered his life to discover it not to anyone, he having already utterly denied it; whereupon both of us stood hovering between joy and fear, yet it continued in silence, and no man made further inquiry about it. Thus in both places we consumed three hours, and now, although it had struck seven, nothing was hitherto given us to eat, but our hunger was abated by constant revivings, and I could be content to fast all my life with such an entertainment. About this time the curious fountains, mines, and all kind Fastidium pulsum of art shops were also shown us, of which there was none egregiis spectaculis. but surpassed all our arts even if melted into one mass. Every chamber was built in semi-circle, that so they might

Officinarum constitutarum finis.

have before their eyes the costly clock-work which was erected upon a fair turret in the centre, and regulate themselves according to the course of the planets which were to be seen on it in a glorious manner. At length I came into a spacious room, in the middle whereof stood a terestrial globe, whose diameter contained thirty foot, albeit near half, except a little which was covered with the steps, was let into the earth. Two men might readily turn it about, so that more of it was never to be seen but so much as was above the horizon. I could not understand whereto those ringlets of gold (which were upon it in several places) served, at which my Page laughed, and advised me to view them more narrowly, when I found there my native country noted with gold also, whereupon my companion sought his and found that too. The same happened to others who stood by, and the Page told us that it was yesterday declared to the King's Majesty by their old astronomer Atlas, that all the gilded points did exactly answer to their native countries, and, therefore, he, as soon as he perceived that I undervalued myself, but that nevertheless there stood a point upon my native country, moved one of the captains to intreat for us to be set upon the scale at all adventures, especially seeing one of our native countries had a notable good mark. And truly it was not without cause that he, the Page of greatest power, was bestowed on me. For this I returned him thanks, and looking more diligently upon my native country, I found that, besides the ringlets, there were also certain delicate streaks upon it. I saw much more even upon this globe than I am willing to discover. Let each man take into consideration why every city produceth not a philosopher. After this he led us within the globe, for on the sea there was a

Globus terrenus.

Excellentia patriæ autoris.

tablet (whereon stood three dedications and the author's name) which a man might gently lift up, and by a little board go into the center, which was capable of four persons, being nothing but a round board whereon we could sit and at ease by broad daylight (it was now already dark) contemplate the stars, which seemed like mere carbuncles glittering in an agreeable order, and moving so gallantly that I had scarce any mind ever to go out again, as the Page afterwards told the Virgin, and with which she often twitted me, for it was already supper time and I was almost the last at table. The waiters treated me with so much reverence and honour that for shame I durst not look up. To speak concerning the musick, or the rest of that magnificent entertainment, I hold needless, because it is not possible sufficiently to express it. In brief there was nothing there but art and amenity. After we had each to other related our employment since noon (howbeit, not a word was spoken of the library and monuments), being already merry with wine, the Virgin began thus:—"My Lords, I have a great contention with one of my sisters. In our chamber we have an eagle, whom we cherish with such diligence that each of us is desirous to be the best beloved, and upon that score have many a squabble. On a day we concluded to go both together to him, and toward whom he should show himself most friendly, hers should he properly be. This we did, and I, as commonly, bare in my hand a branch of lawrel, but my sister had none. As soon as he espyed us both, he gave my sister another branch which he had in his beak, and offered at mine, which I gave him. Each of us hereupon imagined herself best beloved of him. Which way am I to resolve myself?"

This modest proposal pleased us mightily well, and each

Quid in glob.

Reverentia in convivio exhibita auctoris.

The Lady Chamberlain

Perplexed speeches, or intricate questions.

one would gladly have heard the solution, but inasmuch as all looked upon me, and desired to have the beginning from me, my mind was so extreamly confounded that I knew not what to do but propound another in its stead, and said, therefore :—"Gracious. Lady, your Ladyship's question were easily to be resolved if one thing did not perplex me. I had two companions who both loved me exceedingly ; they being doubtful which was most dear to me, concluded to run to me unawares, and that he whom I should then embrace should be the right; this they did, yet one of them could not keep pace with the other, so he staid behind and wept ; the other I embraced with amazement. When they had afterwards discovered the business to me, I knew not how to resolve, and have hitherto let it rest in this manner till I may find some good advice herein."

Autoris griphus.

The Author's counter-demand.

The Virgin wondered at it, and well observed where about I was, upon which she replied, that we should both be quit, and then desired the solution from the rest. But I had already made them wise, wherefore the next began thus—"In my city a Virgin was condemned to death, but the judge being pittiful towards her, proclaimed that if any man desired to be her champion, he should have free leave. Now she had two lovers; one made himself ready, and came into the lists to expect his adversary ; afterwards the other presented himself, but coming too late, resolved nevertheless to fight, and suffer himself to be vanquished that the Virgin's life might be preserved, which succeeded accordingly. Thereupon each challenged her, and now, my lords, instruct me to which of them of right she belongeth." The Virgin could hold no longer, but said :—" I thought to have gained much information, and am my self gotten into

Griphus, 3.

the net ; yet I would gladly hear whether there be any
more behind." " Yes, that there is," answered the third,
" a stranger adventure hath not been recounted then that
which happened to myself. In my youth I loved a worthy Griphus, 4.
maid, and that my love might attain its end I made use of
an ancient matron, who easily brought me to her. Now it
happened that the maid's brethren came in upon us as we
three were together, and were in such a rage that they
would have taken my life, but, on my vehement supplication, they at length forced me to swear to take each of them
for a year to my wedded wife. Now, tell me, my Lords,
should I take the old or the young one first?" We all
laughed sufficiently at this riddle, yet none would undertake to unfold it, and the fourth began. " In a certain Griphus, 5.
city there dwelt an honourable lady, beloved of all, but
especially of a noble young man, who would needs be too
importunate with her. At length she gave him this de-
termination, that in case he would, in a cold winter, lead
her into a fair green garden of Roses, then he should obtain,
but if not he must resolve never to see her more. The
noble man travelled into all countries to find one who might
perform this, till at length he lite upon a little old man who
promised to do it for him, in case he would assure him of
half his estate, which he having consented to the other was
as good as his word. Whereupon he invited the Lady
home to his garden, where, contrary to her expectation,
she found all things green, pleasant, and warm ; and
remembring her promise, she only requested that she
might once more return to her lord, to whom with sighs
and tears she bewailed her lamentable condition. Her
lord, sufficiently perceiving her faithfulness, dispatched her
back to her lover, who had so dearly purchased her, that

she might give him satisfaction, when the husband's integrity so mightily affected the noble man that he thought it a sin to touch so honest a wife, and sent her home with honour to her lord. The little man, perceiving such faith in all these, would not, how poor soever he were, be the least, but restored the noble man all his goods, and went his way. Now, my lords, which of these persons showed the greatest ingenuity?" Here our tongues were quite cut off, neither would the Virgin make any reply but that another should go on; wherefore the fifth began:—

Griphus, 6. "I desire not to make long work. Who hath the greater joy, he that beholdeth what he loveth, or he that only thinketh on it?" "He that beholdeth it," said the Virgin. "Nay," answered I, and hereupon rose a contest till the

7. sixth called out:—"My lords, I am to take a wife; I have before me a maid, a married wife, and a widdow; ease me of this doubt, and I will help to order the rest." "It goes well there," replied the seventh, "when a man hath his

8. choice, but with me the case is otherwise. In my youth I loved a fair and virtuous virgin, and she me in like manner; howbeit, because of her friends' denyal, we could not come together in wedlock, whereupon she was married to another, who maintained her honourably and with affection, till she came into the pains of childbirth, which went so hard with her that all thought she was dead, so with much state and mourning she was interred. Now, I thought with myself, during her life thou couldst have no part in this woman, but dead as she is, thou mayst embrace her sufficiently, whereupon I took my servant with me, who dug her up by night. Having opened the coffin and locked her in my arms, I found some little motion in her heart, which increased from my warmth, till

I perceived she was indeed alive. I quietly bore her home, and after I had warmed her chilled body with a costly bath of herbs, I committed her to my mother until she brought forth a fair son, whom I caused faithfully to be nursed. After two days (she being then in a mighty amazement) I discovered to her all the affair, requesting that for the time to come she would live with me as a wife, against which she excepted thus, in case it should be grievous to her husband, who had maintained her well and honourably, but if it could otherwise be, she was the present obliged in love to one as well as the other. After two months (being then to make a journey elsewhere) I invited her husband as a guest, and amongst other things demanded of him whether if his deceased wife should come home again he could be content to receive her, and he affirming it with tears and lamentations, I brought him his wife and son, recounting all the fore-passed business, and intreating him to ratifie with his consent my fore-purposed espousals. After a long dispute he could not beat me from my right, but was fain to leave me the wife. But still the contest was about the son." Here the Virgin interrupted him and said :—"It makes me wonder how you could double the afflicted man's grief." Upon this there arose a dispute amongst us, the most part affirming he had done but right. " Nay," said he, " I freely returned him both his wife and son. Now tell me, my lords, was my honesty or this man's joy the greater ? " These words so mightily cheared the Virgin that she caused a health to go round, after which other proposals went on somewhat perplexedly, so that I could not retain them all ; yet this comes to my mind, that one told how a few years before he had seen a physitian, who bought a parcel of wood against winter, 9.

with which he warmed himself all winter long; but as soon as spring returned he sold the very same wood again, and so had the use of it for nothing. "Here must needs be skill," said the Virgin, "but the time is now past." "Yea," replyed my companion, "whoever understands how to resolve all the riddles may give notice of it by a proper messenger; I conceive he will not be denied." At this time they began to say grace, and we arose altogether from the table rather satisfied and merry than glutted; it were to be wished that all invitations and feastings were thus kept. Having taken some few turns up and down the hall, the Virgin asked us whether we desired to begin

Virgo lucifera gratiositas.

the wedding. "Yes," said one, "noble and vertuous lady;" whereupon she privately dispatched a Page, and, meantime, proceeded in discourse with us. In brief, she was become so familiar that I adventured and requested her Name. The Virgin smiled at my curiosity, and replyed:—"My name contains five and fifty, and yet hath

Ænigma de Nomine.

only eight letters; the third is the third part of the fifth, which added to the sixth will produce a number, whose root shall exceed the third itself by just the first, and it is the half of the fourth. Now the fifth and seventh are equal, the last and first also equal, and make with the second as much as the sixth hath, which contains four more than the third tripled. Now tell me, my lord, how am I called?"

The answer was intricate enough, yet I left not off, but said:—"Noble and vertuous Lady, may I not obtain one only letter?" "Yea," said she, "that may well be done. "What, then," I proceeded, "may the seventh contain?"

60, Sc. quot virgines.

"It contains," said she, "as many as there are lords here." With this I easily found her Name, at which she was well pleased, saying that much more should yet be revealed to us. Meantime certain virgins had made themselves ready, and came in with great ceremony. Two youths carried lights before them, one of whom was of jocond countenance, sprightly eyes, and gentile proportion, while the other lookt something angerly, and whatever he would have must be, as I afterwards perceived. Four Virgins followed them; one looked shamefully towards the earth; the second also was a modest, bashful Virgin; the third, as she entered, seemed amazed at somewhat, and, as I understood, she cannot well abide where there is too much mirth. The fourth brought with her certain small wreaths, to manifest her kindness and liberality. After these four came two somewhat more gloriously apparelled; they saluted us courteously. One of them had a gown of skeye-colour, spangled with golden stars: the other's was green, beautified with red and white stripes. On their heads they had thin flying white tiffaties, which did most becomingly adorn them. At last came one alone, wearing a coronet, and rather looking up towards heaven than towards earth. We all took her for the Bride, but were much mistaken, although in honour, riches, and state she much surpassed the bride, and afterwards ruled the whole Wedding. On this occasion we all followed our Virgin, and fell on our knees; howbeit, she shewed herself extreamly humble, offering each her hand, and admonishing us not to be too much surprized at this, which was one of her smallest bounties, but to lift up our eyes to our Creator and acknowledge his Omnipotency, and so proceed in our enterprised course, employing this grace to the praise of God and the good of man. In sum her words were quite different from those of our Virgin, who was somewhat more worldly. They pierced even through

[Marginal notes:]
Redduntur pondera choro Virginum.
2 Juvenes.
4 Virgines.
2 Virgines.
1 Virgo præstans.
The Dutchess.

my bones and marrow. "Thou," said she further to me, "hast received more than others ; see that thou also make a larger return."

This to me was a very strange sermon, for as soon as we saw the Virgins with the musick, we imagined we should fall to dancing. Now the Weights stood still in the same place, wherefore the Queen (I yet know not who she was) commanded each Virgin to take up one, but to our Virgin she gave her own, which was the largest, and commanded us to follow behind. Our majesty was then somewhat abated, for I observed that our Virgin was but too good for us, and that we were not so highly reputed as we ourselves were almost willing to phantsie. We were brought into the first Chamber, where our Virgin hung up the Queen's weight, during which an excellent spiritual hymn was sung. There was nothing costly in this room save certain curious little Prayer-Books which should never be missing. In the midst was a pulpit, convenient for prayer, where in the Queen kneeled down, and about her we also were fain to kneel and pray after the Virgin, who read out of a book, that this Wedding might tend to the honour of God, and our own benefit. We then came into the second chamber, where the first Virgin hung up her weight also, and so forward till all the ceremonies were finished, upon which the Queen again presented her hand to every one, and departed with her Virgins. Our president staied awhile with us, but because it had been already two hours night she would then no longer detain us, and, though methought she was glad of our company, she bid us good night, wishing us quiet rest. Our Pages were well instructed, and shewed every man his chamber, staying with us in another pallet, in case we wanted any thing. My chamber was royally furnished

Marginal notes:

Ponderum repositio in locum suum.

The Dutchess.

Reginæ habitatio.

Supellex.

The Dutchess.

Virgo lucifera discedit cubitum.

Puerorum comitum officium.

with rare tapistries, and hung about with paintings; but above all things I was delighted in my Page, who was so excellently spoken, and experienced in the arts, that he yet spent me another hour, and it was half an hour after three when I fell asleep. This was the first night that I slept in quiet, and yet a scurvy dream would not suffer me to rest, for I was troubled with a Door which I could not get open, though at last I did so. With these phantasies I passed the time, till at length, towards day, I awaked.

Autoris thalamus.

Somnium deporta difficili.

The Fourth Day.

I still lay in my bed, and leisurely surveighed the noble images and figures about my chamber, during which, on a sudden, I heard the musick of coronets, as if already they had been in procession. My Page skipped out of the bed as if he had been at his wits' end, and looked more like one dead than living. "The rest are already presented to the King," said he. I knew not what else to do but weep outright, and curse my own sloathfulness. I dressed myself, but my Page was ready long before me, and ran out of the chamber to see how affairs might yet stand. He soon returned with the joyful news that the time was not past, only I had over-slept my breakfast, they being unwilling to waken me because of my age, but that now it was time for me to go with him to the Fountain, where most were assembled. With this consolation my spirit returned, wherefore I was soon ready with my habit, and went after the Page to the Fountain in the Garden, where I found that the Lyon, instead of his sword, had a pretty large tablet by him. Having well viewed it, I found that it was taken out of the ancient monuments, and placed here for some especial honour. The inscription was worn with age, and, therefore,

Autor longiuscule dormiens expergesit.

Jentaculo privatur.

Leonis Tabula.

K

I am minded to set it down here, as it is, and give every one leave to consider it.

HERMES PRINCEPS.
POST TOT ILLATA
GENERI HUMANO DAMNA,
DEI CONSILIO :

ARTISQUE ADMINICULO
MEDICINA SALUBRIS FACTUS
HEIC FLUO.

Bibat ex me qui potest : lavet, qui vult : turbet, qui audet :
BIBITE FRATRES, ET VIVITE.

Scriptura facilis. This writing might well be read and understood, being easier than any of the rest. After we had washed ourselves out of the Fountain, and every man had taken a *Potus.* draught out of an intirely golden cup, we once more followed the Virgin into the hall, and there put on new *Vestitus.* apparel, all of cloth of gold gloriously set out with flowers. There was also given to everyone another Golden Fleece, set about with pretious stones, and various workmanship according to the utmost skill of each artificer. On it hung a weighty medal of gold, whereupon were figured the sun and moon in opposition, but on the other side stood this poesie :—"The light of the moon shall be as the light of the sun, and the light of the sun shall be seven times *Clinodiæ.* brighter than at present." Our former jewels were laid in a little casket, and committed to one of the waiters. After this the Virgin led us out in our order, where the *Musici.* musitians waited ready at the door, all apparelled in red velvet with white guards. After which a door, that I

never before saw open, was unlocked; it opened on the
Royal winding-stairs. There the Virgin led us, together *Accessus*
with the musick, up three hundred sixty-five stairs; we *ad regis aulam.*
saw nothing but what was of extream costly and artificial
workmanship; the further we went, the more glorious still
was the furniture, until at the top we came under a painted
arch, where the sixty virgins attended us, all richly ap- *Laborato-*
parelled. As soon as they had bowed to us, and we as *rium aron-*
atum 60
well as we could had returned our reverence, the musitians *Virgines.*
were dispatched away down the winding-stairs, the Door
being shut after them. Then a little Bell was told, when
in came a beautiful Virgin, who brought every one a wreath
of lawrel, but our Virgins had branches given them. *Virg. Lucif.*
Meanwhile, a curtain was drawn up, where I saw the King
and Queen as they sate in their majesty, and had not the
yesterday queen warned me I should have equalled this
unspeakable glory to Heaven; for besides that the room *Regis et*
glittered of meer gold and pretious stones, the Queen's *Reginæ*
gloria.
robes were so made that I was not able to behold them.
In the meantime the Virgin stept in, and then each of the
other virgins, taking one of us by the hand, with most pro- *Virgo*
found reverence presented us to the King. Whereupon *lucifera*
præsentat
the Virgin began thus to speak:—"That to honour your *hospites*
Regi.
most gratious, royal Majesties, these Lords have adventured
hither with peril of body and life, your Majesties have
reason to rejoyce, especially since the greatest part are
qualified for inlarging your Majesties' dominions, as you
will find by a most gratious particular examination of each.
Herewith I was desirous thus to have them in humility
presented to your Majesties, with most humble suit to discharge me of this my commission, and to take information
from each of them concerning my actions and omissions."

Hereupon she laid her branch on the ground.   It would have been fitting for one of us to have spoken somewhat on this occasion, but, seeing we were all troubled with the falling of the uvula, old Atlas stept forward and spoke on the King's behalf :—" Their Royal Majesties most gratiously rejoyce at your arrival, and will that their grace be assured to all.   With thy administration, gentle Virgin, they are most gratiously satisfied, and a Royal Reward shall be provided for thee ; yet it is their intention that thou shalt this day also continue with them, inasmuch as they have no reason to mistrust thee."

Hospites nesciunt respondere. Atlas respondet.

Here the Virgin humbly took up the branch, and we for this first time were to step aside with her.   This room was square on the front, five times broader than it was long, but towards the West it had a great arch like a porch, where stood in circle three glorious thrones, the middlemost being somewhat higher than the rest.   In each throne sate two persons—in the first sate a very antient King with a gray beard, yet his consort was extraordinarily fair and young.   In the third throne sate a black King of middle age, and by him a dainty old matron, not crowned, but covered with a vail.   But in the middle sate the two young persons, who though they had likewise wreaths of lawrel upon their heads, yet over them hung a large and costly crown.   Now albeit they were not at this time so fair as I had before imagined to my self, yet so it was to be. Behind them on a round form sat for the most part antient men, yet none had any sword or other weapon about him. Neither saw I any life-guard but certain Virgins which were with us the day before, and who sate on the sides of the arch.   I cannot pass in silence how the little Cupid flew to and again there, but for the most part he hovered

Descriptio labatorii.

Subscellia.

1. Rex senex Conjux Juven.

2. Rex and conjux seneᶜ.

Scomna. assessores.

Cupide.

about the great crown. Sometimes he seated himself in
between the two lovers, somewhat smiling upon them with
his bow. Sometimes he made as if he would shoot one of
us ; in brief, this knave was so full of his waggery, that
he would not spare even the little birds, which in multi- Aves.
tudes flew up and down the room, but tormented them all
he could. The virgins also had their pastimes with him, Virgines.
and when they could catch him it was no easie matter for
him to get from them again. Thus this little knave made
all the sport and mirth. Before the Queen stood a small Supellex in
but inexpressibly curious altar, wherein lay a book covered aula altare.
1. Book.
with black velvet, only a little overlaid with gold. By this
stood a taper in an ivory candlestick, which, although very 2. Taper.
small, burnt continually, and stood in that manner, that
had not Cupid, in sport, now and then puffed upon it, we
could not have conceived it to be fire. By this stood a
sphere or celestial globe, which of itself turned about. 3. Sphære.
Next this was a small striking-watch, by that a little 4. Watch.
christal pipe or syphon-fountain, out of which perpetually 5. Little
ran a clear blood-red liquor, and last of all there was a scull Fountain.
or death's head, in which was a white serpent, of such a 6. Scull.
serpent.
length, that though she crept circle-wise about the rest of
it, yet her taile still remained in one of the eye-holes until her
head again entered at the other ; so she never stirred from
her scull, unless Cupid twitched a little at her, when she
slipt in so suddenly that we could not choose but marvel at
it. There were hung up and down the room wonderful
images, which moved as if alive. Likewise, as we were Imagines.
passing out, there began such marvellous vocal musick that Musicæ.
I could not tell whether it were performed by the virgins
who yet stayed behind, or by the images themselves. We, Disceditur
ex labora-
being for this time satisfied, went thence with our virgins, torio

who, the musitians, being already present, led us down the winding stairs, the door being diligently locked and bolted. As soon as we were come again into the hall, one of the virgins began :—"I wonder, Sister, that you durst adventure yourself amongst so many persons." "My Sister," replyed our president, "I am fearful of none so much as of this man," pointing at me. This speech went to my heart, for I understood that she mocked at my age, and indeed I was the oldest of all ; yet she comforted me by promising, that in case I behaved myself well towards her, she would easily rid me of this burden.

Meantime a collation was again brought in, and every one's Virgin seated by him, who well knew how to shorten the time with handsom discourses, but what these and their sports were I dare not blab out of school. Most of the questions were about the arts, whereby I could lightly gather that both young and old were conversant in the sciences. Still it run in my thoughts how I might become young again, whereupon I was somewhat the sadder. This the Virgin perceived, and, therefore, began :—"I dare lay anything, if I lye with him to-night, he shall be pleasanter in the morning." Hereupon they began to laugh, and albeit I blushed all over, I was fain to laugh too at my own ill-luck. Now there was one there that had a mind to return my disgrace upon the Virgin, whereupon he said :— "I hope not only we but the virgins themselves will bear witness, that our Lady President hath promised herself to be his bed-fellow to-night." "I should be well content with it," replyed the Virgin, "if I had not reason to be afraid of these my sisters ; there would be no hold with them should I choose the best and handsomest for myself." "My Sister," presently began another, " we find hereby

Virgines jocantur de senio autoris.

Convivium cum virginibus.

Sermones conviviales.

Autor mæstus ob senium.

Jocosum solatium accipit à Virgine.

Socio.

Virg. lucif.

that thy high office makes thee not proud, wherefore if by
thy permission we might by lot part the Lords here present,
thou shouldst, with our goodwill, have such a preroga-
tive." We let this pass for a jest, and began again to discourse together, but our Virgin could not leave tormenting
us, and continued :—"My lords, how if we should permit *Ludicra electio una dormientium.*
fourtune to decide which of us must be together to-night ?"
"Well," said I, "if it may be no otherwise, we cannot
refuse such a proffer." Now because it was concluded to
make this trial after meat, we resolved to sit no longer at
table, so we arose and each walked up and down with his
Virgin. "Nay," said the president, "it shall not be so
yet, but let us see how fortune will couple us," upon which
we were separated. Now first arose a dispute how the
business should be carried out, but this was only a pre-
meditated device, for the Virgin instantly proposed that
we should mix ourselves in a ring, and that she beginning
to count from herself, the seventh was to be content with
the following seventh, were it a virgin or man. We were
not aware of any craft, and therefore permitted it so to be ;
but when we thought we had very well mingled ourselves,
the Virgins were so subtil that each knew her station
before-hand. The president began to reckon, the seventh
next her was a Virgin, the third seventh a Virgin likewise,
and this continued till, to our amazement, all the Virgins
came forth and none of us was hit. Thus we poor wretches
remained standing alone, and were forced to confess that
we had been handsomely couzened, albeit, whoever had
seen us in our order might sooner have expected the sky to
fall then that it should never have come to our turn.
Herewith our sport was abandoned. In the interim the
little wanton Cupid came also in unto us, but because he

presented himself on behalf of their Royal Majesties, and deliverd us a health from them out of a golden cup, and was to call our Virgin to the King, withal declaring he could not at this time tarry, we could not sport ourselves with him, so, with a due return of our most humble thanks we let him flye forth again. Now because the mirth began to fall into my consort's feet, and the Virgins were nothing

A merry dance.

sorry to see it, they lead up a civil dance which I rather beheld with pleasure then assisted, for my mercurialists were so ready with their postures, as if they had been long

Hospites invitantur a virgine Lucif. ad comediam.

of the trade. After some few dances, our president came in again, and told us how the artists and students had offered themselves to their Royal Majesties before their departure to act a merry comedy ; and if we thought good to be present thereat, and to waite upon their Royal Majesties to the House of the Sun, it would be acceptable to them. Hereupon we returned our humble thanks for the honour vouchsafed us, and most submissively tendered our small service, which the Virgin related, and presently brought word to attend their Royal Majesties in the gallery, whither we were soon led, and staid not long there, for the

Processus Regis ad spectandum comediam.

Royal Procession was just ready, yet without musick. The unknown Queen who was yesterday with us went foremost with a small and costly coronet, apparelled in white satin, and carrying nothing but a small crucifix made of a pearl, and this very day wrought between the young King and his Bride. After her went the six fore-mentioned Virgins in two ranks, carrying the King's jewels belonging to the little altar. Next to these came the three Kings. The Bridegroom was in the midst of them with a plain dress of black sattin, after the Italian mode. He had on a small round black hat, with a little black pointed feather, which he courteously put off to us, thereby to signify his favour towards us. To him we bowed, as we had been before instructed. After the Kings came the three Queens, two whereof were richly habited ; she in the middle went likewise all in black, and Cupid held up her train. Intimation was given us to follow, and after us the Virgins, old Atlas bringing up the rear. Through many stately walks we came to the House of the Sun, there next to the King and Queen, upon a richly furnished scaffold, to behold the foreordained comedy. We, though separated, stood on the right hand of the Kings, but the Virgins on the left, except those to whom the Royal Ensignes were committed. To them was allotted a peculiar standing at top of all, but the rest of the attendants were content to stand below between the columns. Now because there are many remarkable passages in this Comedy, I will in brief run it over.

Statio spectatorum

A Precipuâ quæ agebantur.

First of all came forth a very antient King with some servants ; before his throne was brought a little chest, with mention that it was found upon the water. Being opened, there appeared in it a lovely babe, together with certain jewels, and a small parchment sealed, and superscribed to the King. This the King presently opened, and having read it, he wept and declared to his servants how injuriously the King of the **Moores** had deprived his aunt of her country, and had extinguished all the royal seed even to this infant, with the Daughter of which country he had purposed to match -his Son. Hereupon he swore to maintain perpetual enmity with the Moore and his allies, and to revenge this on him. He commanded that the Child should be tenderly nursed, and to make preparations against the Moore. This provision, and the discipline of the young lady (who after she was a little grown up was com-

Actus 1.

mitted to an ancient tutor), continued all the first act, with
Interludium. many laudable sports beside. In the interlude a Lyon and
Griffon were set at one another, and the Lyon got the
victory; this was also a pretty sight.

Actus 2. In the second act, the Moore, a black, treacherous fellow,
came forth, who having with vexation understood that his
murder was discovered, and that a little lady was craftily
stollen from him, began to consult how by stratagem he
might encounter so powerful an adversary, whereof he was
at length advised by certain fugitives who fled to him
through famine. So the young lady, contrary to all
expectation, fell again into his hands, whom had he not
been wonderfully deceived by his own servants, he had
like to have slain. Thus this act was concluded with a
mervelous triumph of the Moore.

Actus 3. In the third act a great army on the King's part was
raised against the Moore, and put under the conduct of an
antient, valiant knight, who fell into the Moore's country,
till he forceably rescued the young Lady from a tower, and
apparelled her anew. After this they erected a glorious
scaffold and placed her upon it; presently came twelve
royal embassadors, amongst whom the Knight made a
speech, alledging that the King, his most gracious Lord,
had not only heretofore delivered her from death, and
caused her to be royally brought up, though she had not
behaved herself altogether as became her, but, moreover,
had, before others, elected her as a spouse for the young
Lord, his Son, most gratiously desiring that the espousals
might be really executed in case they would be sworn to his
Majesty upon the following articles. Hereupon out of a
patent he caused certain glorious conditions to be read;
the young Lady took an oath inviolably to observe the

same, returning thanks in most seemly sort for so high a grace. Whereupon they began to sing to the praise of God, of the King, and the young Lady, and for this time so departed. In sport, meanwhile, the four beasts of 𝕯𝖆𝖓𝖎𝖊𝖑, Interludium. as he saw them in the vision, were brought in, all which had its certain signification.

In the fourth act the young Lady was restored to her Actus 4. lost kingdom and crowned, being in this array conducted about the place with extraordinary joy. After various embassadors presented themselves not only to wish her prosperity but also to behold her glory. Yet it was not long that she preserved her integrity, but began to look wantonly about her, and to wink at the embassadors and lords. These her manners were soon known to the Moore, who would by no means neglect such an opportunity ; and because her steward had not sufficient regard to her, she was easily blinded with great promises, so that she had no good confidence in her King, but privily submitted herself to the intire disposal of the Moore, who having by her consent gotten her into his hands, he gave her words so long till all her kingdom had subjected itself to him ; after which, in the third scene of this act, he caused her to be led forth, stript naked, and then upon a scurvy wooden scaffold bound to a post, well scourged, and at last sentenced to death. This woful spectacle made the eyes of many to run over. Naked as she was, she was cast into prison, there to expect death by poyson, which, however, killed her not, but made her leprous all over. Thus this act was for the most part lamentable. Between they brought forth 𝕹𝖊𝖇𝖚𝖈𝖍𝖆𝖉𝖓𝖊𝖟𝖟𝖆𝖗'𝖘 image, which was adorned with all manner of arms on the head, breast, legs, and feet, of which more shall be spoken in the future explication.

Actus 5. In the fifth act the young King was acquainted with all that had passed between the Moore and his future spouse, who interceded with his father for her, intreating that she might not be left in that condition, and embassadors were dispatched to comfort her, but withal to give her notice of her inconsiderateness. She, nevertheless, would not receive them, but consented to be the Moore's concubine, and the young King was acquainted with it.

Interludium. After this comes a band of fools, each of which brought a cudgel, wherewith they made a great globe of the world, and undid it again, the which was a fine sportive phantsie.

Actus 6. In the sixth act, the young King resolved to bid battle to the Moore, which was done, and albeit the Moore was discomfited, yet all held the young King for dead, but he came again to himself, released his spouse, and committed her to his steward and chaplain, the first whereof tormented her mightily, while the priest was so insolently wicked that he would needs be above all, till the same was reported to the young King, who dispatched one to break the neck of the priest's mightiness, and adorn the bride in Interludium. some measure for the nuptials. After this act a vast artificial elephant was brought in, carrying a great tower with musitians, which was well pleasing to all.

Actus 7. In the last act the bride-groom appeared in such pomp as is not well to be believed. The bride met him in the like solemnity, whereupon all the people cried out—VIVAT Comædorum SPONSUM, VIVAT SPONSA, so that by this comedy they did applausus erga Regem withal congratulate our King and Queen in the most stately et Reginam. manner, which pleased them most extraordinary well. At length they made some pasces about the stage, till at last they altogether began thus to sing.

I.

This time full of love
Does our joy much approve
Because of the King's Nuptial ;
  And, therefore, let's sing,
  Till from all parts it ring,
Blest be he that granted us all !

Cantilena.

II.

The Bride most exquisitely faire,
Whom we attended long with care,
  To him in troth is plighted ;
We fully have at length obtain'd
The same for which we did contend—
  He's happy that's fore-sighted.

III.

Now the parents kind and good
By intreaties are subdued ;
Long enough in hold was she mew'd ;
  So in honour increase
  Till 𝕿𝖍𝖔𝖚𝖘𝖆𝖓𝖉𝖘 arise
And spring from your own proper blood.

After this thanks were returned, and the comedy was finished with joy to the particular liking of the Royal Persons, who, the evening being already hard by, departed in their fore-mentioned order, we attending them up the winding stairs into the previous hall, where the tables were already richly furnished. This was the first time that we were invited to the King's table. The little altar was placed in the midst of the hall, and the six royal ensignes were laid upon it. The young King behaved himself very gratiously towards us, yet he could not be heartily merry ; he discoursed a little with us, yet often sighed, at which the little Cupid only mocked, and played his waggish tricks. The old King and Queen were very serious, but the wife of one of the ancient Kings was gay enough, the cause

Epilogus.

Hospites invitantur ad cœnam Regis et Reginæ.

Rex Adolesc.

Reges adulti.

whereof I understood not. The Royal Persons took up the first table, at the second we only sate ; at the third some of the principal Virgins placed themselves. The rest were fain to wait. This was performed with such state and solemn stillness that I am afraid to make many words of it. All the Royal Persons, before meat, attired themselves in snow-white glittering garments. Over the table hung the great golden crown, the pretious stones whereof, without other light, would have sufficiently illuminated the hall. All the lights were kindled at the small taper upon the altar. The young king frequently sent meat to the white serpent, which caused me to muse. Almost all the prattle at this banquet was made by Cupid, who could not leave us, and me especially, untormented, and was perpetually producing some strange matter. However, there was no considerable mirth, from whence I could imagine some great imminent peril. There was no musick heard, and if we were demanded anything, we were fain to give short answers, and so let it rest. In short, all things had so strange a face that the sweat began to trickle down over my body, and I believe that the stoutest-hearted man would have lost courage. Supper being almost ended, the young King commanded the book to be reached him from the altar. This he opened and caused it again to be propounded to us by an old man whether we resolved to abide with him in prosperity and adversity, which we having with trembling consented to, he further caused us sadly to be demanded whether we would give him our hands on it, which, when we could fain no reason, was fain so to be. One after another rose and with his own hand writ himself down in this book, after which the little christal fountain was brought near, together with a very small christal glass,

Ordo discumbarium.

Ornatus vestium.

Corona super mensam.

Cupido was the merriest.

Sermones breves.

Oratio Regis adolescentis.

out of which all the Royal Persons drank; afterwards it
was reached to us, and so forward to all, and this was
called the Draught of Silence. Hereupon all the Royal Haustus de
silentio.
Persons presented us their hands, declaring that in case we
did not now stick to them we should never hereafter see
them, which verily made our eyes run over. But our
president engaged herself and promised largely on our Fide jubetur
virg. lucif.
behalf, which gave them satisfaction. Mean time a little
bell was tolled, at which all the Royal Persons waxed so
mighty bleak that we were ready utterly to despair. They
quickly put off their white garments and assumed intirely Mors
Regulorum.
black ones; the whole hall was hung with black velvet, the
floor covered with the same, with which also the ceiling
was overspread. The tables were also removed, all seated
themselves upon the form, and we also had put on black
habits. Our president, who was before gone out, comes in
again, bearing six black taffeta scarffs, with which she
bound the six Royal Persons' eyes, and there were immediately brought in by the servants six covered coffins, which
were set down, a low black seat being placed in their
midst. Finally, there stept in a cole-black, tall man, who
bare in his hand a sharp ax. Now after that the old King Decollatio
Regum.
had been brought to the seat, his head was instantly whipt
off and wrapped in a black cloth, the blood being received
in a great golden goblet, and placed with him in the coffin
that stood by, which, being covered, was set aside. Thus
it went with the rest, so that I thought it would have come
to me too, but as soon as the six Royal Persons were
beheaded, the black man retired, another following who
just before the door beheaded him also, and brought back Carnificis.
his head, which, with the ax, was laid in a little chest.
This indeed seemed to me a bloody Wedding, but, because

I could not tell what the event would be, I was fain to captivate my understanding until I were further resolved.

Hospites mærent.
Solatium.

The Virgin, seeing that some of us were faint-hearted and wept, bid us be content, saying :—" The life of these standeth now in your hands, and in case you follow me, this death shall make many alive."

Herewith she intimated we should go sleep and trouble ourselves no further, for they should have their due right. She bade us all good night, saying that she must watch the

Cura
nocturna
mortuorum.

dead corps. We then were conducted by our Pages into our lodgings. My Page talked with me of sundry matters, and gave me cause enough to admire his understanding, but his intention was to lull me asleep, which at last I observed, whereupon I made as though I was fast asleep, but no sleep came to my eyes, and I could not put the beheaded out of my mind. Now my lodging was directly

Cubiculum.

Visio
nocturna.

over against the great lake, so that I could look upon it, the windows being nigh the bed. About midnight I espied on the lake a great fire, wherefore I quickly opened the window to see what would become of it. Then from far I saw seven ships making forward all full of lights. Above each of them hovered a flame that passed to and fro, and sometimes descended, so that I could lightly judge that it must needs be the spirits of the beheaded. The ships gently approached to land, and each had no more than one mariner. When they were gotten to shore, I espied our Virgin with a torch going towards them, after

Cadavera
avehuntur
trans Lacum.

whom the six covered coffins, together with the little chest, were carried, and each was privily laid in a ship. Wherefore I awaked my Page, who hugely thanked me, for having run much up and down all day, he might quite have over-slept this, though he well knew it. As soon as the coffins were laid in the ships, all the lights were extinguished, and the six flames passed back together over the lake, so that there was but one light for a watch in each ship. There were also some hundreds of watchmen encamped on the shore, who sent the Virgin back again into the Castle, she carefully bolting all up again ; so that I could judge that there was nothing more to be done this night. We again betook ourselves to rest. I only of all _{Autor solus hæc vidit.} my company had a chamber towards the lake and saw this. Then being extream weary I fell asleep in my manifold speculations.

The Fifth Day.

The night was over, and the dear wished-for day broken, _{Obambulatio antelucana.} when hastily I got me out of bed, more desirous to learn what might insue than that I had sufficiently slept. After I had put on my cloathes, and according to my custom was gone down stairs, it was still too early, and I found nobody else in the hall, wherefore I entreated my Page to lead me a little about the castle, and shew me somewhat that was rare, who now (as always) willing, presently lead me down certain steps underground to a great iron door, on which the following words were fixed in large copper letters :—

Thalamus
veneris
sepultæ.

These I copied and set down in my table-book. After this door was opened, the Page lead me by the hand through a very dark passage till we came to a little door now only put too, for, as the Page informed me, it was first opened yesterday when the coffins were taken out, and had not since been shut. As soon as we stepped in I espied the most pretious thing that Nature ever created, for this vault had no other light but from certain huge carbuncles.

Thesaurus
Regis.

This was the King's Treasury, but the most glorious and principal thing was a sepulchre in the middle, so rich that I wondered it was no better guarded, whereunto the Page answered me, that I had good reason to be thankful to my planet, by whose influence I had now seen certain pieces which no humane eye (except those of the King's family)

Descriptio
sepulchri.

had ever viewed. This sepulcher was triangular, and had in the middle of it a kettle of polished copper, the rest was of pure gold and pretious stones. In the kettle stood an angel, who held in his arms an unknown tree, whose fruit continually falling into the kettle, turned into water therein, and ran out into three small golden kettles standing by. This little altar was supported by an eagle, an ox, and a lion, which stood on an exceeding costly base. I asked my Page what this might signifie. "Here," said he, "lies buried Lady Venus, that beauty which hath undone many a great man, both in fourtune, honour, blessing, and prosperity"; after which he showed me a copper door in

Aliud tri-
clinium.

the pavement, saying, "Here, if you please, we may go further down." We descended the steps, where it was exceeding dark, but the Page immediately opened a little chest in which stood a small ever-burning taper, wherefrom he kindled one of the many torches that lay by. I was mightily terrified and asked how he durst do this. He

gave me for answer, " as long as the Royal Persons are still
at rest I have nothing to fear." Herewith I espied a rich
bed ready made, hung about with curious curtains, one of
which he drew, and I saw the Lady Venus stark naked *Descriptio corporis veneris dormientis.*
(for he heaved up the coverlets too), lying there in such
beauty, and a fashion so surprising, that I was almost
besides myself, neither do I yet know whether it was a
piece thus carved, or an humane corps that lay dead there,
for she was altogether immoveable, and yet I durst not
touch her. So she was again covered, yet she was still, as
it were, in my eye. But I soon espyed behind the bed a
tablet on which it was thus written.

I asked my Page concerning this writing, but he laughed,
with promise that I should know it too, and, he putting
out the torch, we again ascended. Then I better viewed
all the little doors, and found that on every corner there
burned a small taper of pyrites of which I had before taken
no notice, for the fire was so clear that it looked much
liker a stone than a taper. From this heat the tree was *Arboris calor ex facibus.*
forced continually to melt, yet it still produced new fruit.
" Now, behold," said the Page, " when the tree shall be

quite melted down, then shall Lady Venus awake and be the mother of a King." Whilst he was thus speaking, in flew the little Cupid, who at first was somewhat abashed at our presence, but seeing us both look more like the dead then the living, he could not refrain from laughing, and demanded what spirit had brought me thither, whom I with trembling answered, that I had lost my way in the castle, and was by chance come hither, that the Page had likewise been looking up and down for me, and at last lited upon me here, and that I hoped he would not take it amiss. " Nay, then, 'tis well enough yet," said Cupid, " my old busie gransir, but you might lightly have served me a scurvy trick, had you been aware of this door. I must look better to it," and so he put a strong lock on the copper door where we before descended. I thanked God that he lited upon us no sooner ; my Page, too, was the more jocond because I had so well helped him at this pinch. " Yet can I not," said Cupid, " let it pass unrevenged that you were so near stumbling upon my dear mother." With that he put the point of his dart into one of the little tapers, and heating it somewhat, pricked me with it on the hand, which at that time I little regarded, but was glad that it went so well with us. Meantime my companions were gotten out of bed and were come into the hall, to whom I joyned myself, making as if I were then first risen. After Cupid had carefully made all fast again, he came likewise to us, and would needs have me shew him my hand, where he still found a little drop of blood, at which he heartily laughed, and bad the rest have a care of me, as I would shortly end my days. We all wondered how he could be so merry and have no sence of yesterday's sad passages. Our President had meantime made herself ready for a journey, coming in

Mulcta facta hujus obambulationis.

Cupido illudit autori.

Mira Cupidinus laetitia.

all in black velvet, yet she and her Virgins still bare their Præsidissæ vestitus iugubris. branches of lawrel. All things being in readiness, she bid us first drink somewhat, and then presently prepare for the procession, wherefore we made no long tarrying, but followed her out of the hall into the court, where stood six coffins, and my companions thought no other but that the six Royal Persons lay in them, but I well observed the device, though I knew not what was to be done with these other. By each coffin were eight muffled men. As soon as the musick went, it was so doleful a tune that I was astonished at it, they took up the coffins, and we followed them into the Garden, in the midst of which was erected a wooden edifice, have round about the roof a glorious crown, and standing upon seven columns. Within it were formed six sepulchers ; by each of them was a stone, but in the middle it had a round hollow rising stone. In these graves the coffins were quietly, and with many ceremonies, laid ; the stones were shoved over them, and they shut fast, but the little chest was to lie in the middle. Herewith were my companions deceived, for they imagined that the dead corps were there. On the top of all was a great flag, having a Phœnix painted on it, perhaps the more to delude us. After the funerals were done, the Virgin, having placed herself upon the midmost stone, made a short oration, Hospites vocantur ad labores pro vita Regum. exhorting us to be constant to our ingagements, not to repine at the pains we must undergo, but be helpful in restoring the buried Royal Persons to life, and therefore, without delay, to rise and make a journey with her to the Tower of Olympus, to fetch thence the medicines necessary for this purpose.

This we soon agreed to, and followed her through another little door to the shore, where the seven ships stood empty, and on them all the Virgins stuck up their Laurel branches, and, having distributed us in the six ships, they caused us in God's name to begin our voyage, and looked upon us as long as we were in sight, after which they, with all the watch-men, returned into the Castle.   Our ships had each of them a peculiar device; five of them, indeed, had the five regular bodies, each a several one, but mine, in which the Virgin too sate, carried a globe.   Thus we sailed on in a singular order, and each had only two mariners.   Foremost went the ship *a* in which, as I conceive, the Moor lay.   In this were twelve musitians who played excellently well, and its device was a pyramid.   Next followed three abreast, *b, c,* and *d,* in which we were disposed; I sate in *c.*   Behind these came the two fairest and stateliest ships, *e* and *f,* stuck about with many branches of lawrel, and having no passengers in them; their flags were the sun and moon.   But in the rear was only one ship, *g,* and in this were forty Virgins. Having passed over this lake, we came through a narrow arm into the right sea, where all the sirens, nymphs, and sea-goddesses attended us, and immediately dispatched a sea-nymph unto us to deliver their present of honour to the Wedding.   It was a costly, great, set, round, and orient pearl, the like to which hath not at any time been seen, either in ours or in the new world.   The Virgins having friendly received it, the nymph intreated that audience might be given to their divertisements, which the Virgin was content to give, and commanded the two great ships to stand into the middle, and to the rest to incompass them in pentagon, after which the nymphs fell into a ring about them, and with a most delicate sweet voice began thus to sing:

Virgines remanent in arce.

$$a$$
$$\|$$
$$b \parallel c \parallel d \parallel$$
$$e \parallel f \parallel$$
$$g \parallel$$

40 Virgines comites.

Excipiuntur à nymphis.

I.

There's nothing better here below
Than beauteous, noble Love,
Whereby we like to God do grow,
And none to grief do move ;
Wherefore let's chant it to the King,
That all the sea therewith may ring.
        We question, answer you !

II.

What was it that at first us made ?
        'Twas Love.
And what hath grace afresh conveigh'd ?
        'Twas Love.
And whence (pray tell us !) were we born ?
        Of Love.
How came we then again forlorn ?
        Sans Love.

III.

Who was it, say, that us conceived ?
        'Twas Love.
Who suckled, nursed, and relieved ?
        'Twas Love.
What do we to our parents owe ?
        'Tis Love.
Why do they us such kindness show ?
        Of Love.

IV.

Who gets herein the victory ?
        'Tis Love.
Can Love by search obtained be ?
        By Love.
How may a man good works perform ?
        Through Love.
Who into one can two transform ?
        'Tis Love.

V.

Then let our song sound,
Till its eccho rebound,
To Love's honour and praise ;
May it ever increase
With our noble Princes, the King and the Queen,
The soul is departed, their body's within.

VI.

And as long as we live
God gratiously give,
That as great love and amity
They bear each other mightily,
So we, likewise, by love's own flame
May reconjoyn them once again.

VII.

Then this annoy Into great joy
(If many thousand younglings deign)
Shall change, and ever so remain.

Autori
perplacent
nymphæ and
cantus.

These having, with most admirable concent and melody, finished this song, I no more wondred at Ulisses for stopping the ears of his companions; I seemed to myself the most unhappy man alive that Nature had not made me too so trim a creature. But the Virgin soon dispatched

The nymphs
rewarded.

them, and commanded to set sail ; wherefore the nymphs, having been presented with a long red scarff for a gratuity, dispersed themselves in the sea. I was at this time sensible that Cupid began to work with me too, which tended little

Autori
desunt adhuc
duo.

to my credit ; but as my giddiness is likely to be nothing beneficial to the reader, I am resolved to let it rest. This was the wound that in the first book I received on my head in a dream. Let every one take warning by me of loitering about Venus' bed, for Cupid can by no means brook it.

Turris
Olympi.

After some hours, we came within ken of the Tower of

Olympus; wherefore the Virgin commanded by the discharge of some pieces to give signal of our approach, and immediately we espyed a great white flag thrust out, and a small gilded pinnace sent forth to meet us, wherein was a very antient man, the Warder of the Tower, with certain Custos guards in white, by whom we were friendly received, and conducted to the Tower, which was situated upon an island exactly square,[1] and invironed with a wall so firm and Structura thick that I counted two hundred and sixty paces over. Dies. On the other side was a fine meadow with certain little gardens, in which grew strange, and to me unknown fruits. There was an inner wall about the Tower which itself was as if seven round towers had been built one by another, yet the middlemost was somewhat higher, and within they all entered one into another. Being come to the gates of the Tower, we were led a little aside on the wall, that so the coffins might be brought in without our notice, but of this the rest knew nothing. We were conducted into the 1. Conclave. Tower at the very bottom, which was an excellently painted laboratory, where we were fain to beat and wash Labores hospitum. plants, precious stones, and all sorts of things, extract their juice and essence, put up the same in glasses, and deliver them to be laid up. Our Virgin was so busie with us, and so full of directions, that she knew not how to give us employment enough, so that in this island we were meer drudges till we had atchieved all that was necessary for restoring the beheaded bodies. Meantime, as I afterwards learned, three Virgins were in the first apartment Virginum. washing the corps with diligence. Having at length almost done our preparation, some broath, with a little

---

[1] See additional note, No. 4.

Cibus.
Potus.

Lectus
tenuis.

Autor
speculatur
cœlum
prosomno.

draught of wine, was brought us, whereby I observed that we were not here for pleasure. When we had finished our day's work, everyone had a mattress laid on the ground for him, wherewith we were to content ourselves. For my part I was not much troubled with sleep, and walking out into the garden, at length came as far as the wall, where, the heaven being very clear, I could well give away the time in contemplating the stars. By chance I came to a great pair of stone stairs leading to the top of the wall, and because the moon shone very bright, I was so much the more confident, and, going up, looked too a little upon the sea, which was exceeding calm. Thus having good opportunity to consider better of astronomy, I found that this night there would happen such a conjunction of the planets, the like to which was not otherwise suddenly to be observed. Having looked a good while into the sea, and it being just about midnight, I beheld from far the seven Flames passing over sea hitherward, and betakeing themselves to the top of the spire of the tower. This made me somewhat affraid; for as soon as the Flames had settled themselves, the winds rose, and made the sea very tempestuous. The moon also was covered with clouds, and my joy ended with such fear that I had scarce time enough to hit upon the stairs again, and betake myself to the Tower, where I laid me down upon my mattress, and there being in the laboratory a pleasant and gently purling fountain, I fell asleep so much the sooner. And thus this fifth day too was concluded with wonders.

The Sixth Day.

Next morning, after we had awaked another, we sate Define together to discourse what might be the wont of things. ortæ dubiæ opiniones. Some were of opinion that the corps should all be in-livened again together. Others contradicted this, because the decease of the ancients was not only to restore life but increase too to the young ones. Some imagined that they were not put to death, but that others were beheaded in their stead. Having talked a pretty while, in comes the Custos. old man, and first saluting us, looks about to see if all things were ready. We had herein so behaved ourselves Pyrotechnia hospitum laudatur. that he had no fault to find with our diligence, whereupon he placed all the glasses together, and put them into a case. Presently come certain youths, bringing ladders, Pueri armiferi. roapes, and large wings, which they laid before us and departed. Then the old man began thus :—" My dear Sons, one of these three things must each of you this day constantly bear about with him. It is free for you to make choice of one of them, or to cast lots." We replied that we would choose. " Nay," said he, " let it rather. go by lot. Hereupon he made three little schedules, writing Sors. on one Ladder, on the second Rope, on the third Wings. These he laid in an hat ; each man must draw, and what-ever he happened on was to be his. Those who got ropes imagined themselves in the best case ; but I chanced on a ladder, which hugely afflicted me, for it was twelve-foot long, pretty weighty, and I must be forced to carry it, whereas the others could handsomely coyle their ropes about them, and as for the wings, the old man joyned them so neatly on to the third sort as if they had grown upon them. Hereupon he turned the cock, and the fountain ran no longer, and we were fain to remove it out of the way.   After all things were carried off, he, taking with him the casket and glasses, took leave, and locked the door after him, so we imagined that we had been

Ascensus in 2 conclave.

imprisoned in this Tower; but it was hardly a quarter of an hour before a round hole above was uncovered, where we saw our Virgin, who bad us good morrow, desiring us to come up.   They with the wings were instantly through the hole; only they with the ropes were in an evil plight, for as soon as ever one of us was up, he was commanded to

Restis difficultas.

draw up the ladder to him.   At last each man's rope was hanged on an iron hook, and he climbed up as well as he could, which indeed was not compassed without blisters. When we were all well up, the hole was again covered, and we were friendly received by the Virgin.   This room was the whole breadth of the Tower itself, having six very stately vestries a little raised and reached by three steps.

Descriptio 2 conclav

In these we were distributed to pray for the life of the King and Queen.   Meanwhile the Virgin went in and out at the little door *a* till we had done.   As soon as our process was absolved, there was brought in through the little door by twelve persons, which were formerly our musitians, a wonderful thing of longish shape, which my companions took to be a fountain, and which was placed in the middle.   I well observed that the corps lay in it, for the inner chest was of an oval figure, so large that six persons might well lie therein one by another.   After this they again went forth, fetched their instruments, and conducted in our Virgin, with her she-attendants, to a most

The little casket.

delicate voice of musick.   The Virgin carried a little casket, the rest only branches, and small lamps or lighted

torches, which last were immediately given into our hands,
and we stood about the fountain in this order.

First stood the Virgin A, with her attendants in a ring Ordo chori
round about, with the lamps and branches *c*. Next stood
we with our torches *b*, then the musitians in a long rank;
last of all, the rest of the Virgins *d*, in another long rank.
Whence the Virgins came, whether they dwelt in the Virgines
unde.
Castle, or were brought in by night, I know not, for their
faces were covered with delicate white linnen. The Quid in
arcula.
Virgin opened the casket, in which was a round thing
wrapped in a piece of green double taffata. This she laid
in the uppermost kettle, and covered it with the lid, which
was full of holes, and had besides a rim, on which she
poured in some of the water which we had the day before
prepared; the fountain began immediately began to run,
and through four small pipes to drive into the little
kettle. Beneath the undermost kettle were many sharp

points, on which the Virgins stuck their lamps, that the
heat might come to the kettle and make the water seeth,
which, when it began to simper, by many little holes at *a*,
fell in upon the bodies, and was so hot that it dissolved
them all, and turned them into liquor. What the above-
said round wrapt-up thing was, my companions knew not,
but I understood that it was the Moor's head, from which
the water conceived so great heat. At *b*, round about the
great kettle, there were again many holes, in which they
stuck their branches, but whether this was done of necessity or for ceremony I know not. However, these branches
were continually sprinkled by the fountain, whence it
afterwards dropt somewhat of a deeper yellow into the
kettle. This lasted for near two hours, the fountain still
running, but more faintly. Meantime the musitians went
their way, and we walked up and down in the room, which
truly was so made that we had opportunity enough to pass
away our time. There were images, paintings, clock-works,
organs, springing fountains, and the like. When it was
near the time that the fountain ceased, the Virgin commanded a golden globe to be brought. At the bottom of
the fountain was a tap, by which she let out all the matter
dissolved by those hot drops (whereof certain quarts were
then very red) into the globe. The rest of the water above
in the kettle was poured out, and so this fountain was
again carried forth. Whether it was opened abroad, or
whether anything of the bodies that was useful yet remained, I dare not certainly say, but the water emptied
into the globe was much heavier than six or more of us
were able to bear, albeit for its bulk it should have seemed
not too heavy for one man. This globe being with much
ado gotten out of doors, we again sate alone, but I, per-

Rami
laures.

Deliciæ in
conclavi.

Gravitas
aquæ.

ceiving a trampling over head, had an eye to my ladder.
After one quarter of an hour, the cover above was lifted, and
we commanded to come up, which we did as before, with
wings, ladders, and ropes, and it did not a little vex me that Ascensus in
3 conclave.
whereas the Virgins could go up another way, we were fain
to take so much toil; yet I could judge there must be some
special reason for it, and we must leave somewhat for the old
man to do too. The hole being again shut fast, I saw the
globe hanging by a strong chain in the middle of the room, in
which there was nothing but windows, with a door between Descriptio
conclavis.
every two, which was covered with a great polished looking-
glass. These windows and looking-glasses were so optically
opposed that although the sun, which now shined exceeding
bright, beat only upon one door, yet (after the windows Artif. optica.
towards the sun were opened, and the doors before the
looking-glasses drawn aside) in all quarters of the room
there was nothing but suns, which by artificial refractions
beat upon the whole golden globe hanging in the midst,
which, being polished, gave such a lustre that none of us
could open our eyes, but were forced to look out at
windows till the globe was well heated, and brought to the Mirac. spec.
desired effect. In these mirrors I saw the most wonderful
spectacles that ever nature brought to light, for there were
suns in all places, and the globe in the middle shined
brighter yet. At length the virgin commanded to shut up
the looking-glasses and make fast the windows to let the
globe cool a little, wherefore we thought good, since we
might now have leisure, to refresh ourselves with a breakfast. This treatment was again right philosophical, and Prandium
philosoph.
we had no need to be afraid of intemperance, though we
had no want, while the hope of the future joy, with which
the virgin continually comforted us, made us so jocond that

we regarded not any pains or inconvenience. I can truly say concerning my companions of high quality that their minds never ran after their kitchen or table, but their pleasure was only to attend on this adventurous physic, and hence to contemplate the Creator's wisdom and omnipotency. After our refection we settled ourselves to work, for the globe was sufficiently cooled, which with toil and labour we were to lift off the chain and set upon the floor. The dispute then was how we were to get the globe in sunder, for we were commanded to divide it in the midst. The conclusion was that a sharp-pointed diamond would be best to do it, and when we had thus opened the globe, there was no redness to be seen, but a lovely great snow-white egg, and it mightily rejoyced us that this was so well brought to pass, for the virgin was in perpetual care least the shell might still be too tender. We stood around about this egg as jocond as if we ourselves had laid it, but the Virgin made it presently be carried forth, and departed herself, locking the door behind her. What she did abroad with the egg, or whether it were privately handled, I know not, neither do I believe it. We were again to pause for one quarter of an hour, till the third hole opened, and we, by means of our instruments, came upon the fourth stone or floor. In this room we found a great copper kettle filled with silver sand, which was warmed with a gentle fire, and afterwards the egg was raked up in it, that it might therein come to perfect maturity. This kettle was exactly square. Upon one side stood these two verses writ in great letters—

O. BLI. TO. BIT. MI. LI.
KANT. I.[1] VOLT. BIT. TO. GOLT.

[1] This letter is omitted in one of the German editions.

On the second side were these three words—

SANITAS. NIX. HASTA.

The third had but this one word—

F.I.A.T.

But on the hindmost part stood an entire inscription, running thus—

QUOD

Ignis : Aer : Aqua : Terra :

SANCTIS REGUM ET REGI-

NARUM NOSTR :

Cineribus

Eripere non potuerunt.

Fidelis Chymicorum Turba

IN HANC URNAM

Contulit.

Aó

Now, whether the sand or egg were hereby meant I leave the learned to dispute. Our egg, being ready, was taken out, but it needed no cracking, for the Bird soon freed himself, looking very jocond, though bloody and unshapen. We first set him on the warm sand, the Virgin commanding Pullus implumis. that before we gave him anything to eat we should be sure to make him fast, otherwise he would give us all work enough. This being done, food was brought him, which Vincitur. surely was nothing but the blood of the beheaded deluted Pascitur sanguine with prepared water, by which the Bird grew so fast under decallatorum our eye that we well saw why the Virgin gave such warning of him. He bit and scratched so devilishly that, could he have had his will upon any of us, he would soon

M

have dispatched him.   Now he was wholly black and wild,

Sanguine
alius Regis
pascitur.

wherefore other meat was brought him, perhaps the blood
of another of the Royal Persons, whereupon all his black
feathers moulted and were replaced by snow-white ones.
He was somewhat tamer too, and more tractable, though
we did not yet trust him.   At the third feeding his feathers
began to be so curiously coloured that I never saw the like

Iridescit.

for beauty.   He was also exceedingly tame, and behaved
himself so friendly with us that, the Virgin consenting, we

Liberatur
vinculis.

released him from captivity.   " 'Tis now reason," she began,
" since by your diligence, and our old man's consent, the
Bird has attained with his life and the highest perfection,
that he be also joyfully consecrated by us."   Herewith she
commanded to bring in dinner, since the most troublesome
part of our work was now over, and it was fit we should
begin to enjoy our passed labours.   We began to make
merry together.   Howbeit, we had still our mourning
cloaths on, which seemed somewhat reproachful to our
mirth.   The Virgin was perpetually inquisitive, perhaps to

Primus
usus ejus.

find to which of us her future purpose might prove serviceable, but her discourse was, for the most part, about
Melting, and it pleased her well when any one seemed

Μεθοδία.

expert in such compendious manuals as do peculiarly
commend an artist.   This dinner lasted not above three-
quarters of an hour, which we yet, for the most part, spent
with our Bird, whom we were fain constantly to feed with
his meat, though he continued much at the same growth.
After Dinner we were not long suffered to digest our food,
for the Virgin, together with the Bird, departed from us,

5. Conclave.

and the fifth room was opened, which we reached after
the former manner, and tendred our service.   In this

Avis
balneum.

room a bath was prepared for our Bird, which was so

coloured with a fine white powder that it had the appearance of milk. It was cool when the Bird was set into it, and he was mighty well pleased with it, drinking of it, and pleasantly sporting in it. But after it began to heat, by reason of the lamps placed under it, we had enough to do to keep him in the bath. We, therefore, clapt a cover on the kettle, and suffered him to thrust out his head through a hole, till he had lost all his feathers in this bath, and was as smooth as a new-born babe, yet the heat did him no further harm. In this bath the feathers were quite consumed, and the bath was thereby turned into blew. At length we gave the Bird air, who of himself sprung out of the kettle, and was so glitteringly smooth that it was a pleasure to behold him. But because he was still somewhat wild, we were fain to put a collar, with a chain, about his neck, and so led him up and down *Vincitur.* the room. Meantime a strong fire was made under the kettle, and the bath sodden away till it all came to a blew stone, which we took out, and, having pounded it, we *Balneum coquitur in* ground it on a stone, and finally with this colour painted *lapidem.* the Bird's whole skin over, who then looked much more strangely, for he was all blew except the head, which remained white. Herewith our work in this story was performed, and we, after the Virgin with her blew Bird was departed from us, were called up a hole to the sixth *6. Conclave.* story, where we were mightily troubled, for in the midst a little altar, every way like that in the King's hall, was placed. Upon it stood the six forementioned particulars, and he himself (the Bird) made the seventh. First of all the little fountain was set before him, out of which he drunk a good draught; afterwards he pecked upon the white serpent till she bled mightily. This blood we received in a golden cup, and poured down the Bird's throat, who was mighty averse from it ; then we dipt the serpent's head in the fountain, upon which she again revived, and crept into her death's head, so that I saw her no more for a long time. Meanwhile the sphere turned constantly on until it made the desired conjunction. Immediately the watch struck one, upon which there was going another conjunction. Then the watch struck two. Finally, whilst we were observing the third conjunction, and the same was indicated by the watch, the poor Bird of himself submissively laid down his neck upon the book, and willingly suffered his head to be smitten off by one of us, thereto

Avis decollatur.

chosen by lot. Howbeit he yielded not one drop of blood till he was opened on the breast, and then the blood spun out so fresh and clear as if it had been a fountain of rubies. His death went to the heart of us, yet we might well judge that a naked bird would stand us in little stead. We

Avis combursitur.

removed the little altar, and assisted the Virgin to burn the body, together with the little tablet hanging by, to ashes, with fire kindled at the little taper, afterwards to cleanse the same several times, and to lay them in a box of cypress wood. Here I cannot conceal what a trick I, with

Jocus.

three more, was served. After we had diligently taken up the ashes, the Virgin began to speak thus :—" My Lords, we are here in the sixth room, and have only one more before us, in which our trouble will be at an end, and we shall return home to our castle to awaken our most gratious Lords and Ladies. Now albeit I could heartily wish that all of you had behaved yourselves in such sort that I might have given your commendations to our most renowned King and Queen, and you have obtained a suitable reward, yet because, contrary to my desire, I have found amongst you these four "—pointing at me and three others —" lazy and sluggish labourators, and yet according to my good-will to all, I am not willing to deliver them to condign punishment. However, that such negligence may not remain wholly unpunished, I purpose that they shall be excluded from the future seventh and most glorious action of all the rest, and so they shall incur no further blame from their Royal Majesties."

In what a case we now were I leave others to consider, for the Virgin so well knew how to keep her countenance that the water soon ran over our baskets, and we esteemed ourselves the most unhappy of all men. The Virgin by one of her maids, whereof there were many always at hand, caused the musitians to be fetcht, who were with cornets to blow us out of doors with such scorn and derision that they themselves could hardly sound for laughing. But it did particularly afflict us that the Virgin vehemently laughed at our weeping, and that there might be some amongst our companions who were glad of our misfortune. But it proved otherwise, for as soon as we were come out at the door the musitians bid us be of good cheere, and follow them up the winding staires to the eighth floor under the roof, where we found the old man standing upon a little round furnace. He received us friendly, and heartily congratulated us that we were hereto chosen by the Virgin; but after he had understood the fright we had conceived, his belly was ready to burst with laughing that we had taken such good fortune so hainously. "Hence," said he, "my dear sons, learn that man never knoweth how well God intendeth him." The Virgin also came running in, who, after she had sufficiently laughed at us, emptied her ashes into another vessel, filling hers again with other

Commodum ejoco.

8. *Conclave.*

Virgo. lucif. ludit cœteros. matter, saying, she must now cast a mist before the other artist's eyes, that we in the mean time should obey the old lord, and not remit our former diligence. Herewith she

7. Conclave. departed from us into the seventh room, whither she called our companions. What she first did with them I cannot tell, for they were not only most earnestly forbidden to speak of it, but we, by reason of our business, durst not

Verus labor sub tecto. peep on them through the cieling. Our work was to moisten the ashes with our fore-prepared water till they became like a very thin dough, after which we set the matter over the fire till it was well heated; then we cast it into two little forms or moulds, and so let it cool a little, when we had leisure to look on our companions through

Labor spurius in 7 conclavi. certain crevises in the floor. They were busie at a furnace, and each was himself fain to blow up the fire with a pipe, till he was ready to lose his breath. They imagined they were herein wonderfully preferred before us. This blowing lasted till our old man rouzed us to work again. We opened our little forms, and there appeared two bright and

Homunculi duo. almost transparent little images, a male and a female, the like to which man's eye never saw, each being but four inches long, and that which most mightily surprised me was that they were not hard, but limber and fleshy as other human bodies; yet had they no life, so that I assuredly believe that Lady Venus' image was made after some such way. These angelically fair babes we laid upon two little sattin cushonets, and beheld them till we were almost besotted upon so exquisite an object. The old lord warned us to forbear, and continually to instil the blood of the

Pascuntur sanguine avis. bird, which had been received in a little golden cup, drop after drop into the mouths of the little images, from whence they apparently encreased, becoming according to proportion much more beautiful. They grew so big that we lifted them from the little cushonets, and were fain to lay them upon a long table covered with white velvet. The old man commanded us to cover them up to the breast with a piece of fine white double taffata, which, because of Pulcherri-mus. their unspeakable beauty, almost went against us. Before we had in this manner quite spent the blood, they were in their perfect full growth, having gold-yellow curled hair, and the figure of Venus was nothing to them. But there was not yet any natural warmth or sensibility in them; they were dead figures, yet of a lively and natural colour; and since care was to be taken that they grew not too great, the old man would not permit anything more to be given them, but covered their faces too with the silk, and caused the table to be stuck round about with torches. Let the reader imagine not these lights to have been of necessity, for the old man's intent was that we should not observe when the Soul entred into them, as indeed we should not have taken notice of it, in case I had not twice before seen the flames. However, I permitted the other three to remain in their belief, neither did the old man know that I had seen anything more. Here-upon he bid us sit down on a bench over against the table. The Virgin came in with the musick and all furniture, and carried two curious white garments, the like to which I had never seen in the Castle. I thought no Vestiuntur. other but that they were meer christal, but they were gentle and not transparent. These she laid upon a table, and after she had disposed her Virgins upon a bench round about, she and the old man began many *leger-de-main* tricks about the table, which were done only to blind. All this Spectatores luduntur. was managed under the roof, which was wonderfully

Descriptio
tecti.

formed, for on the inside it was arched into seven hemispheres, of which the middlemost was somewhat the highest, and had at top a little round hole, which was shut and was observed by none but myself. After many ceremonies stept in six Virgins, each of which bare a large trumpet, rouled about with a green, glittering, and burning material like a wreath, one of which the old man took, and after he had removed some of the lights at top, and uncovered their faces, he placed one of the trumpets upon the mouth of one of the bodies in such manner that the upper and wider part of it was directed towards the fore-mentioned hole. Here

Usus
tubarum.

my companions always looked upon the images, but as soon as the foliage or wreath about the shank of the trumpet

Forti ex
cœlo
veniens.

was kindled, I saw the hole at top open and a bright stream of fire shoot down the tube and pass into the body, whereupon the hole was again covered, and the trumpet removed. With this device my companions were deluded into imagining that life came to the image by the fire of the foliage, for as soon as he received his Soul he twinckled his eyes

Homunculi
animati alio
transfer-
untur.

though scarcely stirring. The second time he placed another tube upon its mouth, kindled it again, and the Soul was let down through the tube. This was repeated upon each of them three times, after which all the lights were extinguished and carried away. The velvet carpets of the table were cast together over them, and immediately a travelling bed was unlocked and made ready, into which, thus wrapped up, they were born, and, after the carpets were taken off them, neatly laid by each other, where, with the curtains drawn before them, they slept a good while.

De. 7 concl.

It was now time for the Virgin to see how the other artists behaved themselves; they were well pleased because they were to work in gold, which is indeed a piece of this art, but not the most principal, necessary, and best. They had too a part of these ashes, so that they imagined that the whole Bird was provided for the sake of gold, and that life must thereby be restored to the deceased. Mean time we sate very still, attending when our married couple would awake, and thus about half an hour was spent. Then the wanton Cupid presented himself, and, after he had saluted *Homunculi excitantur a cupidine.* us all, flew to them behind the curtain, tormenting them till they waked. This happened to them with very great amazement, for they imagined that they had slept from the hour in which they were beheaded. Cupid, after he had *Fuerunt illi qui decol- labantur.* awaked them, and renewed their acquaintance one with another, stepped aside and permitted them to recruit their strength, mean time playing his tricks with us, and at length he would needs have the musick fetcht to be somewhat the merrier. Not long after the Virgin herself comes, and having most humbly saluted the young King and Queen, who found themselves somewhat faint, and having *Conjuges induunt vestimenta ut se con- spiciendos præbeant.* kissed their hands, she brought them the two fore-mentioned curious garments, which they put on, and so stepped forth. There were already prepared two very curious chaires, wherein they placed themselves, and were by us with most profound reverence congratulated, for which the King in his own person most gratiously returned his thanks, and again re-assured us of all grace. It was already about five of clock, wherefore they could make no longer stay; but as soon as ever the chiefest of their furniture could be laden, we were to attend the young Royal Persons down the stairs, through all doors and watches unto the ship, in which they inbarqued, *Conjuges vehuntur trans mare.* together with certain Virgins and Cupid, and sailed so swiftly that we soon lost sight of them, yet they were met, as I was informed, by certain stately ships, and in four

hours time had made many leagues out at sea. After five
of clock the musitians were charged to carry all things
back to the ships, and to make themselves ready for the
voyage, but because this was somewhat long a doing, the
old lord commanded forth a party of his concealed soldiers,
who had hitherto been planted in the wall so that we had
taken no notice of any of them, whereby I observed that this
tower was well guarded against opposition. These soldiers
made quick work of our stuff, so that no more remained to
be done but to go to supper. The table being compleatly
furnished, the Virgin brings us again to our companions,
where we were to carry ourselves as if we had truly been
in a lamentable condition, while they were always smiling
one upon another, though some of them too simpathized
with us. At this supper the old lord was with us, who was
a most sharp inspector over us, for none could propound
anything so discreetly but that he knew how to confute or
amend it, or at least to give some good document upon it.
I learned most by this lord, and it were good that each
would apply himself to him, and take notice of his pro-
cedure, for then things would not so often and untowardly
miscarry. After we had taken our nocturnal refection, the
old lord led us into his closets of rarities, dispersed among
the bulworks, where we saw such wonderful productions of
nature, and other things which man's wit in imitation of
nature had invented, that we needed a year sufficiently to
survey them. Thus we spent a good part of the night by
candle-light. At last, because we were more inclined to
sleep then see many rarities, we were lodged in rooms in
the wall, where we had not only costly good beds but
extraordinary handsome chambers, which made us the
more wonder why we were forced the day before to under-

Musick.

Custos senex

Turris custodita a militibus.

Custos est inspector.

Laus hujus senis.

The old man's closets.

go so many hardships. In this chamber I had good rest, and, being for the most part without care, and weary with continual labour, the gentle rushing of the sea helped me to a sound and sweet sleep, for I continued in one dream from eleven of clock till eight in the morning. Somnium prolixum.

The Seventh Day.

After eight of clock I awaked, and quickly made myself ready, being desirous to return again into the tower, but the dark passages in the wall were so many that I wandered a good while before I could find the way out. The same happened to the rest, till we all meet in the nethermost Hospites deponunt vault, and habits intirely yellow were given us, together vestes lugubres. with our golden fleeces. At that time the Virgin declared to us that we were Knights of the 𝕲𝖔𝖑𝖉𝖊𝖓 𝕾𝖙𝖔𝖓𝖊, of which Salutantur equites. we were before ignorant. After we had made ourselves ready, and taken our breakfast, the old man presented each Donantur a sene. of us with a medal of gold. On the one side stood these words—

AR. NAT. MI. Ars naturæ ministra.

On the other these,

TEM. NA. F. Temporis natura filia.

exhorting us to enterprize nothing beyond and against this token of remembrance. Herewith we went forth to the sea, where our ships lay so richly equipped that it was not well possible but that such brave things must first have been brought thither. The ships were twelve in number, six of ours and six of the old lord's, who caused his to be freighted with well-appointed soldiers. But he betook himself to us in our ship, where we were all together. In Navis, 1. the first the musitians seated themselves, of which the old lord had also a great number. They sailed before us to

Vexilla 12 sign. Navis autoris libra. Horolog.

shorten the time. Our flags were the twelve celestial signs, and we sate in Libra. Besids other things our ship had a noble and curious clock which showed us all the minutes. The sea was so calm that it was a singular pleasure to sail, but that which surpassed all was the old man's discourse, who so well knew how

Facundia senis.

to pass away our time with wonderful histories that I could have been content to sail with him all my life long.

Obyiatio ex arce.

The ships passed on, and before we had sailed two hours the mariner told us that he saw the whole lake almost covered with ships, by which we conjectured they were come out to meet us, which proved true, for as soon as we were gotten out of the sea into the lake of the forementioned

500 naves.

river, there stood in to us five hundred ships, one of which sparkled with gold and pretious stones, and in it sate the King and Queen, with lords, ladies, and virgins of high birth. As soon as they were well in ken of us the pieces were discharged on both sides, and there was such a din of

Applausus.

trumpets, shalms, and kettle-drums, that all the ships upon the sea capered again. As soon as we came near, they brought about our ships together and so made a stand.

Atlas oratione excipit hospites.

Old Atlas stepped forth on the King's behalf, making a short but handsom oration, wherein he wellcomed us, and demanded whether the royal Presents were in readiness. The rest of my companions were in an huge amazement whence this King should arise, for they imagined no other but that they must again awaken him. We suffered them to continue in their wonderment, and carried ourselves as if it seemed strange to us too. After Atlas' oration out

Atlanti respondet senex.

steps our old man, making somewhat a larger reply, wherein he wished the King and Queen all happiness and increase, after which he delivered a curious small casket, but what was in it I know not. It was committed to the custody of Cupid, who hovered between them both. After the oration they again let off a joyful volle of shot, and so we sailed on a good time together, till we arrived at another shore, near the first gate at which I first entred. At this place there attended a great multitude of the King's family, together with some hundreds of horses. As soon as we were come to shore and disembarqued, the King and Queen presented their hands to all of us, one with another, with singular kindness, and so we were to get up on horseback. Here I desire to have the reader friendly entreated not to interpret the following narration to any vain glory of mine, but to credit me that had there been not a special necessity in it, I could well have concealed the honour which was shewed me. We were all distributed amongst the lords, but our old lord and I, most unworthy, were to ride even with the King, each of us bearing a snow-white ensign with a Red Cross. I indeed was made use of because of my age, for we both had long grey beards and hair. I had besides fastened my tokens round about my hat, of which the young King soon took notice, and demanded if I were he who could at the gate redeem these tokens. I answered yes in the most humble manner, but he laughed on me, saying there henceforth needed no ceremony, I was HIS Father. Then he asked me wherewith I had redeemed them. I answered, "With Water and Salt," whereupon he wondred who had made me so wise, upon which I grew somewhat more confident, and recounted how it had happened to me with my Bread, the Dove, and the Raven; he was pleased with it, and said expressly, that it must needs be that God had herein

Marginal notes:

Regiis conjugibus donum affert Cupido.

Honor delatus autori cum sene equitat juxta Regem.

Pater.

Tesseras solvit sale et aqua.

vouchsafed me a singular happiness. Herewith we came to the first gate, where the porter with the blew cloaths waited, bearing in his hand a supplication. As soon as he spied me even with the king, he delivered me the supplication, most humbly beseeching me to mention his ingenuity before me towards the King; so, in the first place, I demanded of his majesty what the condition of this porter was, who friendly answered me, that he was a very famous and rare astrologer, always in high regard with the Lord his Father, but having on a time committed a fault against Venus, and beheld her in her bed of rest, this punishment was imposed upon him, that he should so long wait at the gate till some one should release him from thence. I replied, "May he then be released?" "Yes," said the King, "if anyone can be found that hath as highly transgressed as himself, he must stand in his stead, and the other shall be free. This word went to my heart; conscience convinced me that I was the offender, yet I held my peace and delivered the supplication. As soon as the King had read it, he was mightily terrified, so that the Queen, who, with our virgins and that other queen whom I mentioned at the hanging of the weights, rid behind us, asked him what the letter might signifie; but he, putting up the paper, began to discourse of other matters, till in about three hours we came quite to the Castle, where we alighted and waited upon the King into his hall, who called immediately for the old Atlas to come to him in a little closet, and showed him the writing. Atlas made no long tarrying, but rid out to the porter to take better cognizance of the matter, after which the young King, with his spouse and other Lords, Ladies, and Virgins sate down. Then began our Virgin highly to commend the diligence we had used, and the pains and labour we had un-

Marginalia:

Primus custos. Ob, visam venerem factus portitor.

Autor ejusdem delicterus traditur à portitore.

Actus in Arce.

Virg. lucif.

dergone, requesting we might be royally rewarded, and that
she henceforward might be permitted to enjoy the benefit
of her commission. The old lord stood up too, and attested
the truth of all that the Virgin had spoken, and that it was
but equity that we should on both parts be contented.
Hereupon we were to step out a little ; it was concluded
that each man should make some possible wish, and were
to consider of it till after supper. Meantime the King and Ludus Regis
Queen, for recreation's sake, began to play together. It cum Regina.
looked not unlike chesse, only it had other laws, for it was
the vertues and vices one against another, where it might
be ingeniously observed with what plots the vices lay in
wait for the vertues, and how to re encounter them again.
This was so properly and artificially performed that it were Artificios.
to be wished that we had the like game too. During the
game in comes Atlas again, and makes his report in private,
yet I blushed all over, for my conscience gave me no rest.
The King presented me the supplication to read, the con- Supplicatio
tents whereof were to this purpose : First, the writer wished portitoris
traditum
the King prosperity and peace, and that his seed might be autori.
spread far and wide. Afterwards he remonstrated that the
time was now come wherein, according to the royal promise,
he ought to be released; because Venus was already uncovered
by one of his guests, for his observations could not lie to
to him, and that if his Majesty would please to make strict
and diligent enquiry, in case this should not prove to be,
he would remain before the gate all the days of his life.
Then he humbly sued that, upon peril of body and life, he
might be present at this night's supper, being in good hopes
to spye out the offender and obtain his wished freedom.
This was handsomly indited, and I could well perceive his

ingenuity, but it was too sharp for me, and I could well have endured never to have seen it. Casting in my mind whether he might perchance be helped through my wish, I asked the King whether he might not be released some other way, but he replyed no, because there was special consideration in the business, but for this night we might gratifie his desire, so he sent one forth to fetch him in.

Triclinium preciosissimum.

Mean time the tables were prepared in a spatious room, in which we had never before been, which was so compleat that it is not possible for me to describe it. Into this we

Cupido iratus ob venerem visam ab autore.

were conducted with singular ceremony. Cupid was not present, for the disgrace which had happened to his mother had somewhat angered him. In brief, my offence, and the supplication which had been delivered, were the occasion of much sadness, for the King was in perplexity how to make

Etiam Rex condolet.

inquisition amongst his guests. He caused the porter himself to make his strict surveigh, and showed himself as

Lætitia discumbentium.

pleasant as he was able. Howbeit, at length they began again to be merry, and to bespeak one another with all sorts of recreative, profitable discourses. The treatment and other ceremonies then performed it is not necessary to declare, since it is neither the reader's concern nor serviceable to my design, but all exceeded more in invention than that we were overcharged with drinking. This was the last and noblest meal at which I was present. After the bancket the tables were suddainly taken away, and certain curious chairs placed round in circle, in which we, together with the King and Queen, both their old men, the Ladies and Virgins, were to sit. After this a very handsom Page

Post cœnam obligantur equites legibus suis.

opened the above mentioned glorious little book, when Atlas, immediately placing himself in the midst, bespoke us to the ensuing purpose :—That his Royal Majesty had not yet committed to oblivion the service we had done him, and therefore by way of retribution had elected each of us Knights of the Golden Stone. That it was, therefore, further necessary not only once again to oblige ourselves towards his Royal Majesty, but to vow upon the following articles, and then His Royal Highness would likewise know how to behave himself towards his high people. Upon which he caused the Page to read over these articles :—

I. You, my Lords the Knights, shall swear that you will at no time ascribe your order either unto any Devil or Spirit, but only to God, your Creator, and His hand-maid Nature.

II. That you will abominate all whoredom, incontinency, and uncleanness, and not defile your order with such vices.

III. That you, through your talents, will be ready to assist all that are worthy and have need of them.

IV. That you desire not to employ this honour to worldly pride and high authority.

V. That you shall not be willing to live longer than God will have you.

At this last article we could not choose but laugh, and it may well have been placed there for a conceit. Now, being Privilegia. sworn them all by the King's scepter, we were afterwards, with the usual ceremonies, installed Knights, and, amongst other privileges, set over ignorance, poverty, and sickness, to handle them at our pleasure. This was afterwards ratified in a little chappel, whither we were conducted in procession, and thanks returned to God for it. There I also at that time, to the honour of God, hung up my golden fleece and hat, and left them for an eternal memorial. And because every one was to write his name there, I writ thus :—

Summa Scientia nihil Scire,

Fr. CHRISTIANUS ROSENCREUTZ.

Eques aurei Lapidis.

Anno. 1459.

Others writ differently, each as seemed him good ; after which we were again brought into the hall, where, being sate down, we were admonished quickly to bethink our-selves what every one would wish. The King and his party retired into a little closet to give audience to our wishes. Each man was called in severally, so that I can-not speak of any man's proper wish ; but I thought nothing could be more praiseworthy than, in honour of my order, to demonstrate some laudable vertue, and found that none at present could be more famous and cost me more trouble than gratitude ; wherefore, not regarding that I might well have wished somewhat more agreeable to my-self, I vanquished myself, and concluded, even with my own peril, to free the porter, my benefactor. Being called in, I was first demanded whether, having read the suppli-cation, I had suspected nothing concerning the offendor, upon which I began undauntedly to relate how all the busi-ness had passed, how, through ignorance, I fell into that mistake, and so offered myself to undergo all that I had thereby demerited. The King and the rest of the Lords wondred mightily at so un-hoped for confession, and wished me to step aside a little ; and as soon as I was called in again, Atlas declared to me that, although it were grievous to the King's Majesty that I, whom he loved above others, was fallen into such a mischance, yet, because it was not

Jam postulantur depositiones optionum.

Autor optat liberationem portitoris e gratitudine.

Autor reus confitens.

possible for him to transgress his ancient usages, he knew
not how else to absolve me but that the other must be at
liberty and I placed in his stead ; yet he would hope that
some other would soon be apprehended, that so I might be
able to go home again. However, no release was to be
hoped for till the marriage feast of his future son. This Audit
sententiam.
sentence near cost me my life, and I first hated myself
and my twatling tongue in that I could not hold my
peace; yet at last I took courage, and, because I considered there was no remedy, I related how this porter
had bestowed a token on me and commended me to the
other, by whose assistance I stood upon the scale, and so
was made partaker of all the honour and joy already received. And therefore now it was equal that I should show Laus
beneficii
myself grateful to my benefactor, and was willing gently portitoris.
to sustain inconvenience for his sake, who had been helpful
to me in coming to so high place; but if by my wish anything might be effected, I wished myself at home again,
and that so he by me, as I by my wish, might be at liberty.
Answer was made me, that the wishing stretched not so far, Laudatur
à Rege
yet it was very pleasing to his Royal Majesty that I had
behaved myself so generously, but he was affraid I might
still be ignorant into what a miserable condition I had
plunged myself through this curiosity. Hereupon the
good man was pronounced free, and I, with a sad heart,
was fain to step aside. The rest were called for after me, Reliqui
læti evadunt
and came jocundly out again, which was still more to my
smart, for I imagined no other but that I must finish my
life under the gate. I had also many pensive thoughts Autor melan-
choliat.
running in my head as to what I should yet undertake, and
wherewith to spend the time. At length I considered that Spes.
Metus.
I was now old, and, according to the course of Nature, had

few more years to live, that this anguish and melancholy life would easily dispatch me, and then my doorkeeping would be at an end, and that by a most happy sleep I *Solatium.* might quickly bring myself into the grave. Sometimes it vexed me that I had seen such gallant things, and must be robbed of them; sometimes it rejoyced me that before my end I had been accepted to all joy, and should not be forced so shamefully to depart. Thus this was the last and worst shock that I sustained. During these my cogitations the rest were ready, wherefore, after they had received a good night from the King and Lords, each was conducted into his lodging, but I, most wretched man, had nobody to show me the way, and yet must suffer myself to be tormented. That I might be certain of my future function, I was fain *Autor accipit annulum.* to put on the Ring which the other had worn. Finally, the King exhorted me that, since this was the last time I was like to see him in this manner, I should behave myself according to my place, and not against the Order, upon which he took me in his arms and kissed me, all which I understood as if in the morning I must sit at my gate. After they had all spoken friendly to me, and at last presented their hands, committing me to the divine protection, I was by both the old men—the Lord of the Tower and *Auter dormit cum atlante & sene custode Turris.* Atlas—conducted into a glorious lodging, in which stood three beds, and each of us lay in one of them, where we yet spent almost two, &c.

Here are wanting about two leaves in quarto, and he (the author hereof), whereas he imagined he must in the morning be door-keeper, returned home.

This is the end of this publication.

Any remaining blank pages are for our book binding
requirements and are blank on purpose.

To search thousands of interesting publications like this one,
please remember to visit our website at:

http://www.kessinger.net

CPSIA information can be obtained at www.ICGtesting.com
Printed in the USA
240636LV00015B/9/P